Women are taught, from a young age, to def[...] that women are too timid or insecure to spe[...] are rational actors and understand all too well the ways we are punished for being appropriately assertive. But the cost of not challenging this status quo is a loss of agency. Deb shows how to break free of this double bind by sharing practical advice and personal experiences. A must-read, whether you're a woman in the workplace or a man who works with women.

KIM SCOTT, bestselling author of *Just Work* and *Radical Candor*

From a young age, we women are taught that *power* is a dirty word. So what do we do? We continually give it away. Well, that ends here. This book teaches you how to put power back in your hands, where it belongs.

JULIE ZHUO, cofounder of Sundial and author of *Wall Street Journal* bestseller *The Making of a Manager*

Essential wisdom for every professional, from one of the most successful women leaders in Silicon Valley.

ABIGAIL HING WEN, *New York Times* bestselling author and executive producer of *Loveboat, Taipei*

Because I love my wife and daughters, I want them to fully own their power and manifest it in the world. And because I strive to expand this commitment to human flourishing, I pray that this book blesses all women—and the men who love them in their power.

FRED KOFMAN, author of the bestselling book *Conscious Business*

Fast-paced and full of fresh insights and telling case studies, *Take Back Your Power* is essential reading for any woman executive who wants to take charge of her own destiny and *lead*!

MARK THOMPSON, former CEO of the *New York Times*

Liu is scaling feminine power! With vulnerability, generosity, and deep wisdom, Liu shares the variety of ways she has found to own and build her power. When she adds hidden stories of amazing women leaders and super practical how-tos, the reader can't help but be inspired to shift.

AMY KLEMENT, managing partner at Imaginable Futures

Systemic inequity is a fact, but rarely has a solution been presented that empowers individuals to successfully navigate this reality while refusing to accept the inevitably of social norms and structural biases. *Take Back Your Power* provides a road map that shines a light on the current reality while providing a path forward for personal success and professional growth. I've had the privilege of serving with Deb Liu to witness the power of these insights through her personal example.

BRAD SMITH, president of Marshall University

A remarkable book by a remarkable person. Deb Liu uses her life story and the examples of other successful women, as well as the research literature, to provide practical and actionable advice about how to build power and thrive in a world that is often unfair. Although *Take Back Your Power* is written by a woman for women, Liu's insightful recommendations speak to everyone who has faced imposter syndrome or felt like the person who didn't belong—which is, of course, all of us.

JEFFREY PFEFFER, Thomas D. Dee II Professor of Organizational Behavior at Stanford's Graduate School of Business and author of *7 Rules of Power*

I highly recommend Liu's book *Take Back Your Power* to all women in the workplace, and also to anyone from a group that is disadvantaged or underrepresented in the competitive world of business. Her lessons about embracing power, finding your voice, and making alliances should be required reading for anyone seeking to be more effective in their work. Power is necessary to accomplish your mission, realize your vision, and help make the world a better place. Deb's book is an excellent guide for everyone who feels weak and deserves to be a change-maker.

RAJIV PANT, technology executive at Hearst and former CTO of the *New York Times* and the *Wall Street Journal*

Grab a cup of coffee because you won't be able to put this book down. With *Take Back Your Power*, you get a full arsenal of tools to make your magic shine. Deborah masterfully weaves her own intimate journey and advice together with the rich stories of amazing women, each of whom defines power in her own way, leaving you with vivid anecdotes and insights that will change how you act and see yourself.

FIDJI SIMO, CEO of Instacart

TAKE
BACK
YOUR
POWER

TAKE

BACK

YOUR

POWER

10 NEW RULES FOR
WOMEN AT WORK

DEBORAH LIU

CEO OF ANCESTRY

ZONDERVAN BOOKS

Take Back Your Power
Copyright © 2022 by Deborah Yee-Ky Liu

Published in Grand Rapids, Michigan, by Zondervan. Zondervan is a registered trademark of The Zondervan Corporation, L.L.C., a wholly owned subsidiary of HarperCollins Christian Publishing, Inc.

Requests for information should be addressed to customercare@harpercollins.com.

Zondervan titles may be purchased in bulk for educational, business, fundraising, or sales promotional use. For information, please email SpecialMarkets@Zondervan.com.

ISBN 978-0-310-36488-7 (softcover)
ISBN 978-0-310-36487-0 (audio)

Library of Congress Cataloging-in-Publication Data

Names: Liu, Deborah, 1977– author.
Title: Take back your power : 10 new rules for women at work / Deborah Liu.
Description: Grand Rapids : Zondervan, 2022. | Includes bibliographical references. | Summary: "In Take Back Your Power, president and CEO of Ancestry and former vice president of Facebook Deborah Liu breaks down the stereotypes and double standards that society imposes on women, equipping you with the tools to push back against them and achieve success, both in the workforce and at home"—Provided by publisher.
Identifiers: LCCN 2022004950 (print) | LCCN 2022004951 (ebook) | ISBN 9780310364856 (hardcover) | ISBN 9780310364863 (ebook)
Subjects: LCSH: Women in the professions. | Women executives. | Power (Social sciences)
Classification: LCC HD6054 .L575 2022 (print) | LCC HD6054 (ebook) | DDC 650.1082—dc23/eng/20220405
LC record available at https://lccn.loc.gov/2022004950
LC ebook record available at https://lccn.loc.gov/2022004951

Cover design: Micah Kandros
Cover image: Kitsana1980 / Shutterstock
Interior illustrations: Denise Froehlich
Interior design: Denise Froehlich

Printed in the United States of America

To David

*You are proof positive that the best career (and life)
decision I ever made was who I chose to marry*

To Jonathan, Bethany, and Danielle

*You inspired me to write this book as a reminder
that you have more power than you think*

Contents

Foreword

Sheryl Sandberg

I first met Deb Liu in 2009, when she came into my office to interview for a role on Facebook's consumer monetization team. She had a great track record of building impactful products, and I was immediately impressed with her product knowledge and approach to running teams. After she answered a few of my questions, however, our interview took an unexpected turn. Deb took over the interview and pitched me on a new product that Facebook could build: a marketplace where people could buy and sell to their Facebook communities. It was a bold move. I could have easily decided that Deb was not interested in the role for which she was interviewing. Instead, I told Deb how inspired I was by her vision to connect people through commerce and that, after she did the job we needed her to do, I believed we would build her product.

And that is exactly what happened. Deb did great work in the role we hired her for, leading major projects like Facebook Pay and our first direct response ad project. Every time I saw her, which was fairly often, she would remind me of her initial idea. She did the same with other leaders at Facebook. Seven years later, Deb turned that pitch into Facebook Marketplace: a forum where over one billion people now buy and sell items every month.

Deb's commitment to building great products is matched only by her passion for supporting other women. In 2012 less than 10 percent of product managers at Facebook were women. Deb knew how powerful it would be for those women to come together and share their experiences. She began a series of dinners for women product managers in the Bay Area, which later evolved into Women in Product: a group that provides women PMs a space to network, build new skills, and find support. The community started with just a few women and has since grown to over thirty thousand.

Now Deb has taken all the lessons she's learned in her career and turned them into this incredible book, one that I know will inspire and guide others.

As Deb and I know all too well, being a woman in the workplace has never been easy. From school through our first job interviews, women face bias and systemic barriers that men don't. We have to work harder to be seen as competent. As we gain seniority, we're more and more likely to be the only woman in the room, which can mean we encounter even more bias and scrutiny. Women are also more likely than men to face microaggressions, such as being interrupted or having our judgment questioned. For women with traditionally marginalized identities, including women of color, LGBTQ+ women, and women with disabilities, these experiences are often more frequent and much worse.

Navigating bias and discrimination at work takes an immense toll. It contributes to self-doubt, chronic stress, and burnout. It also has a real impact on women's careers. Since 2015, my foundation, LeanIn.Org, and McKinsey & Company have run the annual Women in the Workplace study—the largest study on the state of women in corporate America. Our data shows that although women's representation has inched upward over the past seven years, persistent gaps remain. Women continue to face a "broken rung" at the first step up to manager: for every 100 men promoted to manager, only 86 women are promoted. This means companies aren't laying the foundation they need for sustained progress at more senior levels. As a result, only one in four C-suite executives are women and only one in twenty-five are women of color.

To make our workplaces truly equal, we need widespread changes to the way we work. We need deep accountability, real allyship, and a fundamental shift in how our culture sees and treats women of all backgrounds. This change is worth fighting for, but it won't happen overnight. Women must look for ways to take back our power and thrive in the system that exists today. Fortunately for all of us, Deb has written a book that tells us how.

Part memoir, part leadership manual, *Take Back Your Power* will enlighten you, inspire you, and at times infuriate you as you reflect on everything women are up against. Deb dives deep into the data on age-old gender stereotypes and bias traps—and the reasons we all need to challenge them. By sharing stories of women who have overcome significant obstacles, from astronauts and venture capitalists to authors and professors, Deb proves that leaning into your authentic self trumps conforming to the expectations of others every single time.

Victory in the battle for fairer, more equal workplaces requires all of us to be both outraged and optimistic. We must be both impatient and in this fight for the long run. It's women like Deb who give me hope. She represents courageous, expansive leadership and lifts up others by sharing her own journey. Every woman can learn from this book. It will fundamentally shift the way you show up at work, making you a stronger, more focused leader, and all of our workplaces will be better for it.

Why You Need
This Book

Iabsently took a step back as I watched them talk in front of me. The noisy hotel bustle faded into the background as I watched them slowly turn the three-way conversation into a one-on-one chat—with me the odd "man" out. I felt the awkwardness of being extraneous.

For several years, I gave the second-day keynote address at the preeminent payments industry conference, Money20/20. More than five thousand industry leaders attended this event. As the head of payments at Facebook, I was the most senior leader representing the company. Before I spoke, our partnerships lead (a man I greatly respected) and I would walk the show floor, getting to know prospective partners and industry leaders. Each time we met someone new, the person would greet us both, only to inevitably shift me aside so that they were in conversation with only him. Eventually, they would physically edge me out of the conversation altogether. I would stand to the side, nodding politely.

Given that the payments industry is male-dominated, the attendees' natural inclination was to think that my colleague was in charge. I didn't want to make the interactions awkward, so I rarely said anything. Then, after I had finished the keynote, everyone would come talk to me because suddenly I was worth talking to. I rationalized this behavior as them playing the odds—that in our industry, the man standing next to me was likely in charge. But I was feeding into the problem. I was giving away my power, permitting them to discount me because of my gender.

One night at a dinner of senior women in tech in New York, we women swapped stories of similar experiences at industry conferences and events. Then and there someone declared, "Screw it. Let's make it awkward. If they're going to assume that we are the assistants, we need to call it out and change their perception." We decided together that each time we let these slights slide, we were allowing the system to continue. We made a pact to call out this behavior when it happened and make it known that women should be leaders equal to men.

Power Is Not a Dirty Word

When you look up *power* in the dictionary, the definition feels mundane. Someone who has power is said to be someone who can "influence the behavior of others or the course of events."[1] Written that way, having power seems like something women should aspire to, for ourselves and our children. We want the lives we lead to matter and have a positive impact on the world.

One day Naomi Gleit and I met with product management leaders to discuss a critical issue touching the whole company, and she didn't say a word during the entire meeting.

Naomi, the vice president of growth and integrity and the head of product management, was the third-most tenured employee at Facebook. She cocreated consumer internet growth hacking, which made Facebook, Instagram, and Messenger what they are today. She went on to raise over $2 billion for charity, and her influence touches the lives of billions of people all around the world.

After our meeting, a couple of people reached out to me asking if Naomi cared. Knowing she did, I later asked her why she didn't speak up.

She replied, "I didn't feel I had the authority."

My heart fell as I listened to her familiar response. I said, "Don't give away your power. If you had said anything, everyone would have fallen in line, and the rest of us would have backed you up."

Naomi was one of the most powerful women I knew. The chief product officer had hand-selected her to lead our over one thousand product managers (PMs), and she took the company from one hundred million users to over three billion. Her actions, both inside and outside of the Facebook offices, have shaped countless lives. Tremendous power rested in her hands, but she couldn't see it.

How many women feel this way?

Why Did I Write This Book?

When I was eight, my mother told me that my sister and I were lucky our father was content with having only girls. I was baffled. "Only?" I asked. I knew I wanted two daughters someday, and I didn't understand why anyone would expect that prospect to disappoint him. My mother explained that every one of his seven living siblings had a son to carry on the family name, but my father only had us. That was the first time I was told—explicitly or implicitly—that I was "only a girl" and that being a girl wasn't good enough. Until that moment, it had never occurred to me that being a girl was second best, that because of my gender, my father would never have something that all Chinese fathers deeply wanted . I felt powerless and frustrated at the unfairness of the situation. I didn't choose my gender, and there was no fixing it, no matter how hard I tried. My father never said anything to my sister or me about a desire to have a boy, but it has sat in the back of my mind from that day on.

I never told my father about that conversation, but I watched for signs that he regretted having only daughters. My mother had two miscarriages during seven years of infertility before the birth of my sister. I wondered obsessively if those had been the sons my father never got to meet. I searched for every scrap of evidence that he didn't feel like he had missed out on anything. I strove to make him proud and even considered not changing my last name upon marriage so that I could carry it on.

Cancer took my father in 2012. He got a chance to hold my youngest, Danielle, and rocked her to sleep as he had done with my older two. We knew his time was limited, but we didn't know how quickly cancer would overtake him. Months later, he lay in hospice, and I brought my five-month-old daughter to see him one last time. I reminisced about learning to crab, fish, and shoot with him. I talked to him about how I wished my kids could know him as they grew up. The last thing he said before the cancer stole his ability to speak was, "Thank you." And in the end, I knew he never wondered if we were good enough to equal sons.

I applied to college knowing I wanted to be an engineer, following in my father's footsteps. When I arrived, I was in for a wake-up call. I remember walking into my introductory physics class—a requirement for engineering—looking around, and seeing very few women in the room. I was surprised. My father was an electrical engineer for the government, and my sister was attending Georgia Tech for her chemical engineering degree. I grew up in a small town, and my father had always encouraged our interest in math and science. I had assumed women and men had an equal desire to go into engineering, not understanding the underlying dynamics that resulted in only 25 percent of my fellow graduates being women.[2] Today in the US, even though women earn 27 percent of engineering degrees, they make up less than 16 percent of practicing engineers.[3] When asked why they leave the field, most women cite that they feel like they don't belong. Men and women achieve similar results in college, but women say they feel alienated in group projects and dismissed in the workplace.[4]

My dream of having two daughters did eventually come to pass. I'm the proud mother of two daughters, ages ten and thirteen, and a son, age sixteen. As children their age do, they constantly fight about fairness. Who gets to pick the next show we watch? Who gets the last cookie? So-and-so got to do such-and-such last time, so I should get to do it this time. It's only fair, after all. What they don't realize is that the world has a power imbalance they know nothing about. As children, they live in a world where everything is parsed out in three equal parts, and each of them gets the same slice. But real life is much more complicated. Hidden beneath our society is an undercurrent that inevitably skews in males' favor in every area that matters—in the workplace, in the home, in the government—even in a world that ostensibly supports gender equality. The laws may have women and men on more or less equal footing. There's no debating that. But the challenges begin where the legal definitions end.

How many accomplished, undeniably successful women like Naomi Gleit have had their achievements brushed off by a man? What about a male coworker? A male boss? How many girls have grown up planning to get married, have children, and be home-makers not because they wanted to but because that was what was expected of them? How many lives have been affected by ideas of "should"? *I should stay quiet since others know the space better. I should step carefully because I don't want to be seen as difficult or demanding. I should not apply because I don't meet all the require-ments. I should, I should, I should . . .*

These are the insidious ways of thinking that made even a woman like Naomi feel like she couldn't participate in a meeting with her peers. These deeply ingrained thought patterns and beliefs are tightly woven into the way we interact with the world, stemming from deep social dynamics, and observing them at work was what inspired me to write this book.

I wrote this book for anyone who grew up assuming she was competing equally with her male counterparts, only to come face-to-face with the reality of being a woman, whether in her career or in her relationships.

I wrote this book for anyone who feels herself pushing against a world that gives her less credit for accomplishing the same things as a man . . . and then tells her that her confusion and frustration are all in her head.

I wrote this book for anyone who is told that *power* is a dirty word, that it's best to leave the leading and climbing to the guys, that seeking to change the world is churlish and uncouth.

I wrote this book for all the women who don't know there is a way to rebalance the equation and to take back our power but silently wish there was.

This book is a guide to changing yourself while changing the world. It will teach you to make your mark and take back the power that is rightfully yours.

A Note on "The System"

Women have less power in the world than men, and I write this book accepting this as an immutable truth of our situation. We live in a world where women make up only 20 percent of Russell 3000 company board seats,[5] where for every one hundred men promoted or hired into management, only 86 women are,[6] where women earn six in ten of the college degrees but make less money.[7] This is not a guide to changing that system head-on. That's a problem that will take years of policy changes and activism to address. Instead, I write this book to help women see the invisible bias built into the system around them and teach them to thrive within it even as they fight it. The truth is that we have to live within this system for years to come because it is not changing anytime soon. We can rage against what is, but if we don't understand it and evolve to succeed in it, we will not be able to change it.

The first thing that any of us can do—that any of us *must* do before we can fix a broken system—is to understand the bias at the heart of that system. We must learn how to win, even on an uneven playing field. Is it fair? No. Is it the reality we live with? Yes. We can choose to ignore it, or we can adapt and learn. We must first fight on an individual basis not only to stop giving away our power but also to become comfortable seeking and living with power. That's what this book is for.

Let's take back our power—together.

Know Your Playing Field

The most common way people give up their power is by thinking they don't have any.

—Alice Walker

---

power

|ˈpou(ə)r|

noun

1. the capacity or ability to direct or influence the behavior of others or the course of events
2. physical strength and force exerted by something or someone[1]

The Truth about Women and Power

Women's relationship with power is an interesting and often unbalanced one when compared with men's. In the end, it often comes down to a single ugly truth: women are punished for wanting power, while men are praised for it. Women, on average, make between 10 and 20 percent less than men in the same occupation.[2] Statistically, women also ask for raises as often as men but are 25 percent less likely to get one.[3]

Girls are called bossy, and boys are praised as leaders. We ask our daughters to do more chores and pay our sons more allowance.[4] Teachers invest more time talking to boys, and they allow boys to speak first and more frequently.[5] Boys are taught to compete, and girls are typically taught to nurture.[6] And through all this, we send a message about a girl's place in society.

These expectations are so entrenched that we often don't notice them even as we feed into them. In many small ways, we signal to girls that they are valued more for helping and tell boys they are valued more for leading. A 2010 study from the *Personality and Social Psychology Bulletin* found that participants of both genders reacted differently to power-seeking men and women in political office. Study participants were given a fictional biography of a state senator, with only the name and gender changed. Power-seeking male politicians were seen favorably by both genders, while power-seeking female politicians were seen negatively and went as far as to evoke "feelings of moral outrage."[7] Even though the biographies were identical, the reaction was different simply because of the gender of the subject.

Women are seen with suspicion when they seek power, whereas men are lauded for the same behavior. Men are rewarded for showing up as strong and powerful, while women are expected to be warm and emotionally open. Hillary Clinton's first presidential campaign is a perfect illustration of this. In 2008, after coming in third in Iowa to Barack Obama and John Edwards, she went on to campaign in New Hampshire as the underdog. During a campaign stop at the Café Espresso, a voter asked Clinton, "How do you do it?" Clinton stopped and shared her heartfelt thoughts about how important the campaign was to her personally.[8] Her winning New Hampshire was credited to that moment of vulnerability.

I spoke to a friend who was a high-ranking official in the Clinton campaign in September 2016. Citing studies about women and leadership, I asked if her staff would try to get Clinton to show a hint of her vulnerability this time around. Many reporters and staff who followed Clinton shared stories of her humor and natural leadership, but these qualities didn't show up on the campaign trail when she was in public. I found this contradiction baffling until I read the Humans of New York Facebook page, where Clinton shared how she fought for her place in law school during the draft for the Vietnam War. She was strongly criticized during the exam by the male test-takers around her because they felt she was stealing a spot that could protect a man from being drafted. This experience, and many like it, taught her to protect herself and curb her feelings as a defense mechanism in a male-dominated field, even though it made her seem "walled off."[9]

All of this puts women in a double bind: overtly seek power and be judged harshly for it, or serve quietly and be praised. As Secretary of State under President Obama, Clinton's approval rating was in the high 60s, but when she ran for the highest office in the country, it plummeted to less than 50 percent.[10] There were many reasons why she lost the 2016 election, but as a woman who sought power, she undeniably had to fight against our society's inclination to judge women like her negatively.

Women Don't Seek Power Because We Tell Them Not To

Even now, as you work your way through this book, many of you will feel cognitive dissonance when you see the word *power*. I know this because I remember how I felt when I started writing this book. The word sits heavy on the page. It feels egocentric, self-serving, and ugly, especially when applied to women. We are taught to be good girls, to not ask for too much or be too demanding, either at home or work. Seeking power is antithetical to everything we teach girls.

Mark Zuckerberg, founder and CEO of Facebook, posted his personal challenge for 2016: to build an AI for his home. One of the top comments came from a woman named Darlene Hackemer Loretto, who wrote, "I keep telling my granddaughters to date the nerd in school, he may turn out to be a Mark Zuckerberg!"

Zuckerberg responded, "Even better would be to encourage them to *be* the nerd in their school so they can be the next successful inventor!"[11] Darlene's comment reflects what we teach our girls: they should marry the inventor, not be the inventor.

How many grandparents and parents share Darlene's point of view? My mother used to tell me that she prayed that my sister and I would be *wen rou*, a Chinese word that means "demure" or "graceful." My mother came to America, a country she had never been to, for college. She had a couple of suitcases and knew almost no one. She built a life here from nearly nothing, and she is one of the fiercest women I know. My grandmother never had a formal education, raised seven children, and led my grandfather's company after his death, even though she had limited literacy. Yet even these women, incredibly strong and powerful women in their own right, wanted their daughters to be gentle and demure, fitting into the stereotypes they imagined. This baffled me, hearing the powerful and successful women in my life ask me to tone down my strong personality to be more appealing to a potential husband.

The journal *Science* published a study that demonstrates this bias even in young children. Researchers read a story to hundreds of five-to-seven-year-olds about someone who was "really, really smart" and asked the children to pick a photo of the person in the story. Most five-year-olds picked someone of their own gender, but the six- and seven-year-old boys and girls identified men more often than women as the protagonist.[12] Something happens between ages five and six that signals to girls that women are less smart than men, even though girls outperform boys in nearly all subjects and also graduate with more than half the college degrees awarded in the US.[13]

Women Don't Seek Power Because We Tell Them They Aren't Good Enough

A 2016 study cited in *Harvard Business Review* revealed that our ways of judging leadership potential differ based on sex. Men are seen as leaders if they are competent, while women are seen as leaders if they are competent and warm.[14] This double standard is perhaps what parents are preparing their girls for when they set these expectations of sweetness and gentleness. Teaching them to be nice, helpful, and collegial helps them get ahead because competence alone is insufficient for girls to be taken seriously. Warmth is a prerequisite for influence and power in the workplace; thus, all the lessons about being nice to others are an attempt to show our girls a reality they will later face.

I once took my kids to the library in Palo Alto to check out some chapter books. On the shelves were books that played straight into adult gender stereotypes. The "girl" books were all about princesses, sewing, and keeping diaries, while the "boy" books were about mystery, exploration, and adventure.[15] "Girl" books were about connection and friendship, and "boy" books were about problem-solving and expanding horizons. The subtle messages kids receive give them a sense of who they are expected to be and what they need to do to conform to the world they live in.

In response to what I saw that day, I wrote a middle-grade book with my children about a spoiled princess with a lot to learn, a dragon with a scientific bent, and a failed squire with something to prove, who go off to save the world together. They use brains instead of brawn, and their adventure teaches them that an accident of birth does not dictate their paths in life. In the book, the dragon is often mistaken for a boy dragon. She quips, "Seriously, has no one heard of a girl dragon?"

It took nearly three years to complete my novel, and as we were coming up with a title, my son, Jonathan, pulled me aside and said earnestly, "Mommy, let's not use Sophie's name or the fact she is a princess in the title because the book will be less appealing to boys if it is an adventure about a girl. The point is to have more boys read this, right?"

I groaned but conceded his point. Boys are culturally depicted as leaders, and girls as their sidekicks. Male names appear in 36.5 percent of children's book titles, versus only 17.5 percent for female names.[16] Girls are taught to read adventures about boys, but boys are acculturated to envision themselves as the hero. Bending to this reality, we named the book something gender-neutral to ensure that middle-grade boys would pick it up.

Making accommodations in publishing to appeal to a broader audience is not unusual. All three Brontë sisters wrote under male pseudonyms during the mid-nineteenth century, and since then, publishing has not changed as much as we would like.[17] When J. K. Rowling was working on publishing the Harry Potter books in 1997, her publisher asked to use her initials rather than her name to hide the fact she was a woman.[18] They felt this would help the books to be more appealing to children of both genders.

Women are subtly told from a young age that they aren't good enough simply by virtue of their gender. This message extends to the corporate ladder. Though women earn a majority of all college degrees, they hold less than 10 percent of senior executive roles.[19] Many companies attribute this to a pipeline problem, blaming the fact that there aren't enough women entering the field (the "pipeline") who are qualified to take on these roles. They claim that is why there is no diversity at the top. In reality, women outnumber men in college and enter the workforce close to equal ground in pay, but the pay gap grows as they reach peak childbearing age and then goes down close to retirement age.[20] This gap is largely attributed to the impact of childbearing and rearing. But it also means that women aren't given the first, critical step in growing their careers—becoming a manager for the first time. This stumble on the first rung of the management ladder has lasting consequences. A 2021 survey from McKinsey in partnership with LeanIn.org revealed that for every one hundred men who are promoted to a managerial role, only eighty-six women are. This ratio is even smaller for Black and Latina women.[21]

Women are not offered these positions for a variety of reasons, but one such reason is that they themselves feel unprepared. I remember when a couple of women on my team were returning from parental leave after the birth of their second children. I offered each of them a manager role on the team where they had previously been individual contributors (ICs). Both were unsure. I respected their passion for being ICs, but I sensed that something else was holding them back. Each expressed doubt about her ability to juggle having a newborn and a young child alongside the demands of management. Over several weeks I had a series of conversations with each of them. We explored what their paths would look like, how they could have an impact as managers, and how their careers would evolve. Ultimately, each said yes, and their teams grew and thrived under their leadership. The same happened when I offered the role of engineering manager to the most senior woman engineer on one of my teams. She had just gone through a divorce and couldn't travel, so she asked us to look at other candidates. I spent several months looking but hadn't found someone suitable. Her home life had settled down, and she agreed to step into the role and grew to become a strong leader within the organization.

How many managers would have persisted after the first "no"? I wanted the best person for the job, and I was willing to wait for these talented women to be ready because they were the most qualified candidates, but many managers take resistance at face value and move on to their second candidate, thus leaving the most qualified candidate—often a woman—behind.

Women Don't Seek Power Because Our Words Signal That They Don't Belong

Working in tech for the past twenty years, I have been steeped in the language of an industry where men outnumber women by a significant margin. One day I heard myself talking about a startup as "two guys in a garage," and I stopped short. I realized I reflexively used gender-specific words in everyday conversation without much thought on their impact. That day, I committed to noting every time I noticed or used one of these words in a work context. What started as a brief document grew over the next several months to an expansive list. I was surprised by how deep our gender-specific language runs. These words were not said with misogynistic or negative intent, but rather they were used in innocuous ways.

Words matter, and they affect us whether we realize it or not. Language subtly pushes us to imagine a certain type of person in a role, and it also discourages those who don't fit that image. A 2011 study found that the gendering of everyday language can impact an individual's judgments, decisions, and behavior, influencing both their self-perception and interactions with others.[22]

Once I started documenting these words, I heard them everywhere—in meetings, hallway conversations, and presentations. Many of the masculine phrases, like *manpower* and *right-hand man*, were neutral to positive, usually indicating a position of strength, while nearly all the feminine ones, like *prima donna* and *Debbie Downer*, were negative and indicated weakness. These subtle sexist messages are all around us, and as a mother of a boy and two girls, I wonder what it says to them about the world we live in.

If someone says a project is a "two-man job," who comes to mind for the opportunity? When you hear, "Who is the quarterback on this?" do you instinctively pick someone who fits that description? We are acculturated by language, and this creates an uneven playing field.

A study from the University of Waterloo and Duke University showed that masculine language is widely used in more male-dominated fields, whereas feminine language is not used more often in female-dominated fields.[23] When shown job listings that sounded more masculine, women tended to find them less appealing and sensed they wouldn't belong. Using terms like *gentlemen's agreement* or *manning up* has a subtle but meaningful effect on the workplace.

Women respond to these subtle clues by opting out because they feel less of a sense of belonging. We create spaces for men and then ask why women don't join, or if they do join, they drop out.

Masculine Words

- two-man rule
- man-on-man defense
- gentlemen's agreement
- old boys' club
- man up
- ballsy
- two guys in a garage (beginning a startup)
- right-hand man
- that's his boy
- poster boy
- man bites dog
- manpower
- wingman
- white man's burden
- straw man
- key man risk
- everyman
- middleman
- great man myth
- grow a pair
- big boy pants
- cowboy
- guys
- dude
- man-hours
- quarterback
- manning a booth
- everyone and their brother

Feminine Words

- run like a girl
- spunky
- resting b--- face
- mean girls
- diva
- prima donna
- sassy
- drama queen
- Would your mom be able to use this product?
- mom replacement apps
- mom jeans
- Debbie Downer
- negative Nancy / negative Nelly
- open the kimono

How many times have you heard, "I would hire more diverse teams, but I don't want to lower the bar"? Think about what that implies—that diversity and inclusion necessarily mean reducing the quality of employees. But statistically, if the distribution of talent cuts across all genders and races, then opening an opportunity to more candidates means that you have access to a larger pool and thus a better chance of finding someone who meets your job requirements. When leadership says this, they signal to their company that those who are different are of lower quality and therefore do not belong in the organization.

These signals add up. A female intern shared how she was repeatedly told by her male computer science classmates, "You only got the interview at Facebook and Google because you are a woman." Her jealous classmates implied she was not good enough for the job, that her gender gave her a leg up over them.

When I was invited to the board of Intuit, many people told me that I was fortunate to be a woman, since many board seats are going to women and minorities nowadays. I knew they meant well, but a part of me wondered if they thought I was invited to serve solely because of my identity and not because of what I could contribute. As with that intern, the message to me was that a woman gets opportunities only because of her gender, not because she is the most qualified. After serving on the board for over a year, I finally worked up the courage to ask if they had nominated me for the position just based on my identity. Spoiler alert: They didn't.

The boardroom is one of the least diverse places in the workplace. Women occupy less than 25 percent of the board seats in the Fortune 500, and between 2016 and 2018, 60 percent of new board seats went to men.[24] Even after the state of California passed a mandate that every company headquartered there had to have at least one woman board member, women were appointed to only 45 percent of the new board seats in the first quarter of 2021.[25] At this pace, we will never reach equality in company boards.

This exclusion happens all around us, but much of it is not as overt as the boardroom of public companies. In 2014, Amazon built a résumé screening system that would filter through applications and bring forth high-quality candidates.[26] Trained on ten years of internal data, the system ended up with gender-biased results. It filtered out two women's colleges completely and penalized résumés that included women's activities. Though the system wasn't built with gender discrimination in mind, the algorithm picked up on what hidden criteria recruiters had used to filter out résumés for the last ten years and served them biased results. Separately, Mark J. Girouard, an employment attorney, evaluated a system for a client only to find that the algorithm had two main factors that drove the output: being named Jared and having played high school lacrosse.[27]

These anecdotes may initially seem to point to rogue algorithms until you think more deeply about how they came about. These algorithms merely reflect the choices made by tens of thousands of people over long periods. These choices are then coded into systems that take the initial biases and extend them to new groups of people. It is not the tools that are biased, but rather the inputs. They take years of human decision-making and reveal our biases by breaking down the patterns recruiters and hiring managers have created—patterns we can't see. The experience of one woman would never have uncovered this type of bias, but at scale, it is visible. These biases illustrate how recruiting and promoting employees has made the playing field uneven. No wonder women feel like they don't belong.

Women Don't Seek Power Because We Hold Them to Different Standards

One day I was hosting a women's town hall with Mike Schroepfer, Facebook's chief technology officer, when he mentioned being told—for the first time in his career—to smile more in his talks. He realized that this was something women were told all the time. We went on to discuss how women must conform to specific expectations—both consciously and unconsciously—in a way that men don't.

Threading the needle as a woman in the workplace means you are constantly adapting to fit into the mold of what success looks like, without stepping over an invisible line. This is the subtle tax on being a woman, and although it's invisible, it's real. You must be likable but competent, friendly but firm, helpful but assertive. And there is a cost to not meeting expectations.

A 2014 study found that women were given substantially more critical feedback than men in performance reviews; in particular, there was significantly more "negative personality criticism," which cited a woman's tone or personal style as a problem. Women are called "abrasive," "emotional," and "bossy."[28] We've begun to use shorthand like "poor culture fit," which is just a euphemistic way of saying, "You are not like the rest of us." In fields dominated by men, these expectations put women at a major disadvantage.

Ami Vora, vice president of product and design at WhatsApp, spent nearly two decades as an influential product leader. Early in her career in tech, she received repeated feedback about what she should change to soften her edges and become more relatable and effective. This feedback weighed on her, so she took it to heart and changed herself to conform to the expectations of her managers and peers. Several years later she received feedback that she seemed to blend into the background and didn't have a voice. This is the contradiction that many women face. They are asked to tone down their personalities, to play nice with others, and be less aggressive, but when they do, what remains is often less effective. Ultimately, Ami chose what she would change and what would remain , even if that sometimes felt imperfect. Her predicament, however, is all too common.

The double bind of being a woman in the workplace also extends to venture capital. For two years, researchers from the Luleå University of Technology observed decision-making meetings by Swedish government venture capitalists and entrepreneurs. During the time of observation, women founders were funded less often (47 percent of the time versus 62 percent of the time), and if they were given funding, they received only about a quarter of their ask versus half for their male counterparts.[29] But most interesting was the language used to describe the founders. Youth in men was viewed as promising, whereas it was described as inexperience in women. Caution in men was praised, while it was seen as a detractor for women. These stereotypes crept into the room and were observed by researchers. How often do these unconscious biases affect everyday dealings?

As of 2019 only 2.8 percent of venture capital was invested in companies with all-women founders. Female and mixed-gender teams received only 11.5 percent of all investment. This is a major increase from previous years, but all-male teams still received 88 percent of all venture money.[30] These numbers are not surprising if you look at venture capital and see that only 11 percent of those doing the investing are women.[31] A study by Boston Consulting Group and MassChallenge showed that teams with one or more female founders raised less than half the money compared with their male counterparts, but generated 10 percent more revenues. Thus they are more efficient and effective with their funds.[32] If venture capital were truly equal, a significantly larger share of investments would be distributed to mixed-gender- or female-founded startups since they outperform, but instead, we tell ourselves we live in a meritocracy, even though the data says differently.

Mauria Finley, a successful tech founder and CEO, once told me she liked to pitch male venture capitalists (VCs) who had daughters. I asked her why. She replied, "In VC, investors are conditioned to look for patterns that have made money before. Think 'young male computer science grad' or 'dropout in a hoodie.' They have way fewer 'patterns' for successful women founders."

Interestingly, men in senior positions at these influential venture firms are more likely to hire women into their firms if the men themselves have daughters. These women, in turn, help generate higher returns.[33] Presumably many of these men are married to women whom they view as equals, and being parents forces them to think about the challenges their daughters will one day face. Perhaps this generates a desire to support the women their daughters will one day be.

While most women will never work in tech or become founders, the VC industry is a glimpse into a world where people invest purely for returns yet systematically underestimate half the population. I once had breakfast with an entrepreneur in residence (EIR) at a major VC firm. After holding several senior executive positions at venerated tech companies, she joined the firm as an EIR to explore starting her own company, but she also helped them source and vet deals. She shared her frustration at how the firm summarily dismissed women founders who came to pitch, only to double down on "bros" who were similar to them. She said that the partners sought charisma and passion, gravitating toward the kind of people they would want to hang out with. Many of the women founders presented realistic plans and disciplined execution but were too different from the investors to connect with them. She subsequently left and started a successful tech company of her own.

Another area where we see this double standard is in hiring for traditionally male occupations, where bias against women is strongest. One study in France showed how these closed doors foster bias in outcomes.[34] Forty hiring committees were asked to take implicit bias tests. They were asked to react quickly to words like *male* and *science* to see if they made innate connections between the two more strongly than between *female* and *science*. They were then surveyed about their attitudes about biases against women. Though many of these committees exhibited bias in the test, those who recognized the biases and challenges women face hired more women than those who didn't acknowledge them.

Another study looked at the hiring for academic positions by a university.[35] During the study period, they filled 174 positions, meeting with four candidates on average. If only one of the candidates was a woman, then she had statistically *no chance of being hired*, even though in a candidate pool of four, her normal chances would have been 25 percent. When there were two women in the pool, however, the likelihood of one of them being chosen for the role shot up to 50 percent. Surprisingly, when there was only one male candidate, he had a 33 percent chance of being hired.

Hiring is not neutral. It is the result of individual and collective decision-making multiplied by millions of hiring decisions. Most of the time, it's not the result of overt discrimination. Rather, it's the result of implicit bias, which tilts attitudes toward what we consider the norm. Play this out at a societal level, and it's no wonder the playing field is not level.

Expectations and Motherhood

I had three kids, each one while working at a different tech company. Each time, multiple people asked, "Are you going to come back?" During all three of my pregnancies, at least a few of my own team members asked if I planned to return. Several times when I said I would come back to work, I was asked who would take care of my children.

I mentioned these incidents to my husband after the birth of our third child, and he laughed and said, "Not a single person asked me either one of those questions for any of the kids." My husband has had a similarly successful career at tech companies large and small, and we have traded off being the primary breadwinner over the years. But there is an expectation of mothers that does not exist for fathers.

Whether we like it or not, women are held to different standards than men, as managers, colleagues, and parents. Men and women make about the same salary before the birth of their first child. After giving birth, women's earnings in the US take a long-term hit of over

30 percent. In fact, in a study of six western countries, mothers saw a reduction in earnings, no matter how progressive the society. This ranged from 21 percent in the most egalitarian countries to over 60 percent in the least.[36]

This is not only about discrimination. It is about the interaction of the competing requirements of home and work. Women take on the bulk of the household management, which eventually takes its toll. In the workplace, leaders highly value workers who have the flexibility to be on the company clock, but that is not possible with children at home. Companies are willing to pay a premium to have workers available to collaborate on projects or do last-minute work for clients. That means that there is value placed in being able to work on weekends or after hours or to travel unexpectedly.[37] This pressure only increased with the COVID-19 crisis, when schools and daycares closed. Mothers took on the vast majority of household chores and homeschooling, even in families where both parents worked.

When asked about this, nearly half of fathers said they were the primary teacher for homeschooling during COVID, but only 3 percent of mothers agreed. Eighty percent of women surveyed said they did the bulk of the homeschooling during the pandemic.[38] My husband and I have a fairly balanced household since both of us have worked throughout all three children's childhoods. Even still, I'm considered the "default parent" for schooling.

Maternal bias is one of the most severe of all biases in the workplace. A woman who puts participation in the parent-teacher association on her résumé is 79 percent less likely to be hired.[39] Even if she is hired, she is offered around $11,000 less in salary because she is seen as less serious about her job. If she has a job, she is less likely to be promoted.[40] A study by Stanford researchers showed that women who signaled they were mothers on their résumés were viewed as less competent than child-free women or men with or without children. Yet in our society, more than two-thirds of mothers work outside the home, and in 40 percent of households with children, mothers are the primary or sole breadwinner.[41]

When couples become parents for the first time, men see a fatherhood bonus; women see a motherhood penalty. Men achieve an average 6 percent increase in salary for each child they have, whereas women see a 4 percent loss.[42] Simply put, motherhood puts women at a disadvantage in their careers.

Working in a demanding industry as a mother of three was a balancing act for me. I discussed this with my manager, Doug Purdy, when I returned from maternity leave after the birth of my third child. I had hit a low point where I wasn't sure I could balance it all. Danielle, my third child, never learned to breastfeed, so I pumped for three to four hours a day, and then either my husband or I had to feed her from a bottle. She had colic for nearly a year and cried for two to three hours a night. At the same time, we were renovating our house, my father's cancer had spread to his brain, and he had just entered hospice. Amid all this, I was tasked with building out a new line of business at Facebook for mobile monetization. I asked for Doug's advice on how to juggle all this, and he pointed out that while many women who were our peers had husbands with equally demanding jobs, our male peers were more likely to have a spouse who was managing the home and family. He asked that I not be so hard on myself and instead helped me to find a balance. He allowed me to take time off that I needed to spend with my father. In 2012 Anne-Marie Slaughter wrote the viral article "Why Women Still Can't Have It All." In 2015 Andrew Moravcsik spoke about this challenge in his essay written in response, "Why I Put My Wife's Career First." He wrote, "A female executive needs what male CEOs have always had: a spouse who bears the burden at home."[43]

This wasn't the first time I almost gave up and left this unbalanced playing field. Right after my son, our first child, was born, I reached a turning point in my career. Frustrated with the lack of opportunity at work and the challenge of working in tech while managing a household, I went to Dana Stalder, a vice president at PayPal at the time, and told him I was resigning to stay at home. I had climbed as far as I felt I could reach, and I felt stuck. My career, once promising, had stopped growing, and I knew I was treading water without a chance to advance or take on something new. This feeling of stagnation is something that happens a lot to women in tech. According to a 2008 *Harvard Business Review* study, women leave tech jobs at four times the rate of men, partly due to how they are treated at work and partly because of the challenges of the second shift at home. This exodus is particularly prevalent when women are in their thirties. It's a period when the natural arc of a career opens up doors to leadership positions, but it's also when family responsibilities are at their peak.[44]

The next week, Dana arranged for me to take on a new role of leading the buyer experience product at eBay, so I jumped at the chance to do something new. It turns out I ended up sticking it out there as well as at PayPal, but each time I had a moment of reckoning when I wondered whether the extra effort to stay on the uneven playing field was worth it. For many women, it isn't.

We can pretend the world is fair. We can ignore the mines on the field. We can assume that circumstances will be different for us. I lived under those illusions throughout school and even after I entered the workforce. Then, slowly, I began to see the pitfalls, traps, and biases that were all around me, sometimes long after I had stepped into them.

This first chapter is meant to disappoint you, upset you, and frustrate you. It is meant to make you feel powerless in the face of a world that is unfair. Because for the rest of this book, we will talk about how to take on this unequal playing field, adapt to it, and even thrive within its constraints. All the while, we will learn to push back against the boundaries, speak up even when it's uncomfortable, and take back our power together.

Don't Give Yourself a Free Pass

If they don't give you a seat at the table, bring a folding chair.

—Shirley Chisholm

I once arrived late to a meeting at my company. I realized when I entered the room that eighteen male executives, and not a single woman, were already seated. For a moment, I stood by the door, frozen. Finally, I made my way over to a makeshift stool off to the edge of the group. Even after working in tech for over eighteen years, I had moments like this when the words *you don't belong* flashed through my mind.

When another woman walked in, she came around to where I sat and nudged me toward a seat closer to the CEO. I reluctantly shifted closer to the center, and she claimed the stool on the periphery I had been sitting on.

As an Asian American woman in the tech field, I had the feeling

I didn't belong. I can't hide, and I can't be anything but what I am. I've walked into every room with my differences written on my face. But the weight of expectations is also there, whispering in the background: *Speak up, but don't be aggressive. Be nice but also assertive. Don't make others uncomfortable, but don't back down.*

In rooms where I felt out of place or different, I sought to hide, to be less visible. I weighed every word, wondering if I would accidentally say the wrong thing. What I didn't realize at the time was that, by choosing to stay on the periphery rather than risk rocking the boat, I was giving away my power.

Women face a double standard, and this double standard makes it harder for us to speak up. That means when the opportunity arises, it's even more important that we take advantage of it. There is a great deal of pressure *not* to make ourselves appear aggressive, even though this trait is accepted—and even admired—in our male counterparts.

Rather than giving in to the forces around you, this chapter will encourage you to push back against wrongdoing, call it out, and learn to thrive despite it. I will show you why you can't give yourself a "free pass": permission to stay silent out of fear of judgment, or simply because it's easier.

Speaking Up and Speaking Out

I have often been the "only." The only woman, the only minority, or both. Having grown up in a place where people of Asian origins made up only 1 percent of the population, I learned to hide well to avoid being singled out.

Though I was born in Queens, New York, my family moved to a small town near Charleston, South Carolina, when I was six years old. I was painfully shy and awkward. Moving to a place where many people had never met someone who looked like me branded me as a foreigner and made me feel even more isolated.

My family and I were seen as outsiders in our closed community, and classmates relentlessly bullied me for being different. People came up to our family on the streets and told us to "go back to where we came from." We received prank calls with people mimicking Chinese, our house was egged, and our windows were broken. When I worked up the courage to tell my teachers or administrators, they always told me, "It's not that bad," or, "It's just a few bad people." This went on through my entire childhood, all the way until I graduated high school.

I resented my parents for moving us from New York, where much of our family lived, to this small town where I lived in fear. Over time I learned not to draw attention to myself. Becoming invisible ensured that people didn't notice or taunt me.

One night during high school, I was studying with a friend in my family room when the song "Part of Your World" from *The Little Mermaid* came on the radio. We decided that night that we would earn scholarships to go to college, move on to a world that was far away from our hometown, and never look back. I thought that being where people accepted who I was would solve my problems.

I went on to study engineering at Duke University on a scholarship, where much of the work we did was rather solitary in nature. I spent hundreds of hours in computer labs and working on problem sets. This suited me fine since I enjoyed the individual work and nearly silent study groups where we helped each other through hours of written exercises. I considered going into engineering after I graduated, but at the time, many Duke engineering students were breaking off into consulting or banking, and working on business problems seemed more intellectually appealing to me.

When I was graduating from college, a job in strategy consulting was highly prized. As one of the firm partners at the renowned Boston Consulting Group said to me during the interview process, "For a fresh graduate, joining BCG is like gold-plating your résumé." The group selected the top students from the best schools, and getting a job at this small group of firms was harder than getting into many colleges.

I joined the Atlanta branch of the BCG. I was a good synthesizer of information, wrote comprehensive decks, and crafted strong narratives. I thought that was enough. But consulting is a profession built for those willing to speak up. When I was admonished to "socialize more with the clients," I remember asking my managers, "What does socializing have to do with my competence as an associate?" I noticed that what had worked for me up until that point was no longer working. Being good at problem sets, tests, and group projects meant nothing when it came to the workplace. I had assumed designing better strategies and more beautiful presentation decks were what counted, so I gave myself a free pass and told myself that connecting with clients—the thing I hated—was not important.

After a couple of years, I left the consulting world to attend Stanford Graduate School of Business. I took an organizational behavior class there that focused on how companies and relationships within organizations worked. It covered the important factors of leadership as well as how people interact based on their unconscious biases.

Included in the final exam was the following question: What will you change as a result of being in this class?

I hesitated for a moment and then wrote, "I will be an extrovert at work."

I naively believed during my consulting years that being

successful was about the work produced, but now I understood that part of the impact was building relationships and being present, and hiding my point of view stood in the way of that. I stopped giving myself the free pass to stay comfortable and invisible.

When I graduated I joined a small startup called PayPal as a product manager. From day one I forced myself to change. I spent time investing in relationships, and I was more engaged with those around me. I spoke up in meetings, invited people to lunch, and took the time to speak one-on-one with people throughout the company. I worked outside my comfort zone ten hours a day. It was exhausting at first, but I gradually noticed a change in my way of interacting with others, which in turn affected their responses to me.

By going out of my way to spend time with others, I saw my relationships blossom and grow. When I was practically invisible, as I had been up until that point, I relied on others to draw me out of my shell to get what they needed. By opening up, I connected with others more readily.

I accepted a job at Facebook knowing the expectation was to share openly with my colleagues and that friending your coworkers was the norm. Because of the relatively flat organization, influence came through relationships. Initially, the company functioned on an internal version of Facebook that was tied to your personal account, and posting your thoughts was the way you connected with others and amplified the work of your team.

Facebook, unlike more traditional companies, worked like the social network itself. There was a hidden network of connections and influence that I initially couldn't see or understand. Successfully delivering products meant selling your ideas, getting people on board, and building a coalition of colleagues who wanted to see them come to life. The company allowed employees to shape their roles and also move around to different teams, so a great idea that could get people excited garnered more resources and thus a higher probability of success.

At first, the thought of having to constantly put myself out there paralyzed me, and I was terrible at it. I was accustomed to getting an allocation of resources and deciding on a road map, not constantly advocating and fighting for mindshare and support. But my onboarding mentor, Justin Osofsky, kept pushing me to set up time with people and share my ideas. He kept asking how we could press harder and amplify our work. I realized then that I was failing at the core of my job, which was to do whatever it took to bring my product to life. I had accidentally given myself a free pass.

The Danger of the Free Pass

The concept of a "free pass" came from Carol Isozaki, a well-known Silicon Valley executive coach and leadership trainer. It is something she has taught for over two decades to tens of thousands of people—especially women. A free pass is the act of giving ourselves permission to give away our power.

There is an old adage often attributed to Wayne Gretzky: "You miss 100 percent of the shots you never take."[1] That is the heart of the free pass. You let the ball go by and don't grab it to take a shot.

Carol calls this employing "unintentional ridiculous strategies." No one shows up to a meeting and says to themselves, "I plan to add no value by being here," or, "I plan to suck the energy out of the room." But by giving yourself a free pass, that is exactly what you do, whether you intend to or not.

Hearing Carol speak passionately about not giving yourself a free pass, one would never guess that she grew up painfully shy.

Today she speaks to crowds of hundreds or even thousands, but she started her journey looking inward. The turning point in her life happened because of the guy behind the counter at her favorite pizza place. Carol worked at Musicland, a short distance away, and often went to the pizza place for lunch. One day, the server asked her, "Why do you always look sad or mad?" That moment helped Carol see herself from the outside. She had given herself a free pass, not knowing and taking responsibility for the effect her shyness had on others. Rather than making excuses about how she was born introverted, she decided she would have a positive effect on others, especially her colleagues and clients. This was the first step in tearing up her free pass and making every interaction count.

How many times have you looked outside yourself and seen how others see you? How many times have you had an idea but were too afraid to say it? How many times have you been afraid to ask for a promotion or raise? How many times have you let your male colleague interrupt you and not spoken up? Each time one of these things happens, you give up your power by giving yourself permission not to take the shot. You are giving yourself a free pass.

We women tend to speak up only at the right moment or wait until we have the perfect answer before jumping in. Carol points out, "As a shy person and perfectionist, I assumed 100% of what mattered were the words, and I couldn't come up with how to word it perfectly so I didn't speak. It took me a long time to realize how crazy risky that approach was. Later, I saw the research that words make up only 7% of what is perceived when we speak. I wished I had learned it much earlier so it wouldn't have taken me so long to realize that I was leaving so much influence behind."[2] Professor Albert Mehrabian's research from decades ago had shared that, in communicating feelings or attitudes, the words we use make up a small part of what is perceived. Rather, 55 percent comes from body language, and 38 percent is conveyed by tone.[3] Being present and speaking up is not about coming up with the perfect words; it is about nonverbal communication as well. This realization prompted Carol to stop giving herself a free pass and speak up more—and to do so with the passion she had kept hidden for so long.

Pratiti Raychoudhury is the head of research for Facebook. One day several years ago, we were leading a team focused on scaling out our developer platform. During our biannual review with the executive staff, as I was presenting how our half had gone, the chief operating officer (COO) asked a question about the developer net promoter score. This was something that Pratiti had pioneered and implemented. I nudged her, and she turned and whispered the answer. I shared it with the group by repeating it out loud. Afterward, the COO walked up to me and said, "Never let her do that again. She should speak about her own work, not tell you so you can say it for her."

Pratiti, one of the first researchers hired at Facebook, not only helped shape the function at Facebook but also pioneered the model of research as a core part of product development at technology companies all over the world. In that moment, however, she gave herself a free pass to not speak up.

Each time you enter a room, you leave something of yourself behind. Imagine it as a photograph that you leave on the table. What impression did you want to make? Many people, women in particular, attend a meeting and spend the whole time sitting back and listening, never uttering a word. They leave behind a faded picture, sometimes so blurry that no one knows they were even there. These women invested time in the meeting only to get up and leave without making an impact.

Don't give yourself a free pass. If you are going to show up, make sure you really show up. I can hear the arguments running through your head right now: "I'm an introvert" or "I don't want to say the wrong thing."

But being present means being *heard*.

I spent most of my life in silence, never speaking up in class or at work. But there comes a point in your life when what worked before will stop working, and you have a choice to make: adapt or stagnate. When I arrived at business school, that was a critical moment for me. In most courses, 30 to 50 percent of our grades came from class participation. No longer could I rely solely on turning in perfect assignments and studying hard for the tests, a strategy that helped me graduate as valedictorian from high school and summa cum laude from college. Instead, I had to change my approach. I could have told myself that I was a natural introvert and given myself a free pass. Instead, *I treated speaking up as a learned skill.*

Every week, I set a goal of how many times I would participate in each class and wrote it down on the corner of my notebook. Then I rated myself each time I spoke. This way I could control both the quantity and quality of my responses. At first I struggled. I raised my hand and my comments felt stale, like poorly devised echoes of what someone else had said. But as time went on, I grew quicker, more agile in my comments, more engaged in the dynamics of the conversation. Though it took me over a year, I reached a place where I felt comfortable speaking up, and I no longer experienced fear the same way I did in the beginning.

Not giving yourself a free pass means reframing every obstacle as a learning experience. For me, the most important thing was an impetus. I needed a reason to change. The risk of failing business school was the catalyst. I needed to learn strategic extroversion, so I did.

Speaking Up against the Tide

Dr. Ellen Ochoa flew on the NASA shuttle *Discovery* in 1993 and made history as the first Latina woman in space. That was the first of four trips. She later went on to become the director of NASA's Johnson Space Center. But as a child, she never imagined she would be a trailblazer in space exploration.

Women and minorities were not even selected to be astronauts until Ellen was in college. Then, during her time at Stanford as a PhD student in engineering, Ellen watched Sally Ride become the first American woman in space. Sally had a physics degree just like she did. Ellen saw the potential to follow in Sally's footsteps, so she applied to NASA. It took five years before she was accepted.

When I met Ellen, she was the guest at the Facebook Women's Leadership Day, where thousands of women from all over the world gathered. She shared a story that stuck with me: the story of how she stood her ground, not knowing if she was right or wrong.

As they prepared for their first launch after the tragic loss of the *Columbia* shuttle, which broke up as it reentered the atmosphere in 2003, the team at NASA noticed an issue with some sensors in an external tank. Multiple failure signals required launches to be scrubbed as they investigated the issue. Then came a countdown in which everyone on the mission management team voted "Go" even though a sensor had failed. Ellen represented the crew and decided to vote "No Go," forcing yet another launch to be scrubbed. They called off the launch because of her vote.

The next time they prepared to launch, all the sensors were clear. The shuttle launched successfully and safely.

Even though she was the lone voice of dissent, Ellen did not give herself a free pass. Instead, she stood up and stopped the launch despite everyone else voting against her. Because the team still didn't understand the cause of the failure and therefore couldn't determine the risk it presented, she followed the existing flight rule that called for standing down in the interest of the safety of the crew. It took over a year of investigation, but NASA eventually discovered the source of the issue, which could have affected any of the sensors and thus carried a higher risk than a single failure.

Your Kryptonite and Your Superpower

I will let you in on a secret: in that room where you are different, where you are nothing like anyone else, you have a superpower. What you think is a liability is really a strength. Being different feels fraught, but it allows you to see what many other people can't see. That is a gift. But if you let your voice be silenced because of your discomfort, you risk your difference becoming your kryptonite, the thing that holds you back.

Ellen saw that launching a shuttle with an unknown sensor failure was not a risk worth taking, especially on the heels of the *Columbia* shuttle loss. She realized she had a responsibility to make sure her voice was heard. If your instinct is to say no when everyone else is saying yes, trust that perspective and explain your reasoning.

When you are different from those around you, your point of view will often seem out of step with those of others. But that is precisely why it is so important. Giving yourself a free pass to avoid speaking up means you may miss a vital opportunity. Rather than framing your input as intrusive and contrary, treat it as Ellen did: as additional information that needs to be heard.

When I first joined Facebook in 2009, I participated in a tradition called Hackathon. These events allowed employees to spend a few days working on a side project. Successful projects were pitched to the executives for integration into our main experience. I did my first Hackathon project with Meg Sloan, the company's first user researcher, and Sarah Smith, the head of online operations. Meg and I were two of the few moms at the company at a time when the average employee was under thirty. Our project was based on the idea of letting women announce their pregnancy on Facebook by setting their status to "expecting."

I brought it to the product manager who led the Facebook profile group, and he asked, "Why would anyone want to do that?"

I replied, "What is the first thing you do when you're pregnant and you want to share the news with your friends at week twelve?"

He seemed baffled. "What?"

I said, "You post an ultrasound photo announcing your pregnancy."

Facebook later introduced Major Life Events, which included important milestones users could announce to their friends, including "expecting." Six years later, when the PM's wife was pregnant with their first child, we met up after not having worked together in a while. I reminded him of how we first met. He apologized, and we had a good laugh together.

Eventually, I told this story at my tenth Faceversary, during sharing time at the company-wide Q&A. I shared how diverse points of view can help us build better products for the world. I spent a decade building products and teams that others didn't want to work on or thought wouldn't work. I zigged when others zagged. I looked for projects that no one else wanted to work on and invested in them because I saw something others didn't. Taking the nontraditional path gave me a chance to build several multibillion-dollar businesses, new products that touch people's lives, and a chance to change the course of the company.

It is when you are most afraid of being wrong because your point of view is different that you need to listen to that voice and trust it. Bring your perspective to the fore. That thing you see that others miss will feel obvious to you. You will not understand why others don't see or understand it. Do not shut down your voice to fit in.

Creating Your Own Doors

There will be points in life when you are at a disadvantage, when the odds are stacked against you. You can choose to accept your circumstances, or you can fight to make your own path.

Miriam Rivera attributes much of her success to "the sense of possibility" that her faith, the kindness of others, and the work ethic modeled by her mother gave her throughout her life. Despite a difficult upbringing, she never allowed stumbling blocks to keep her from achieving her potential because she saw there was something greater ahead. She grew up poor, where many around her never escaped the gravitational pull of poverty, but she wanted more. She went on to cofound one of the most influential Latina-led VC funds in Silicon Valley: Ulu Ventures.

Her story starts before she was born.

Miriam's mother grew up in a household in Puerto Rico filled with violence and poverty. Her mother's challenges with depression were exacerbated by having one of her children forcibly taken from her and put up for adoption. She kept her next child, Miriam's older sister, and eventually married, going on to have four more children, including Miriam.

As migrant farm workers, the family had little to live on, so they decided to move to Chicago, Illinois, to become factory workers. But Miriam knew little peace growing up. Her father was physically and verbally abusive. With five children to support, her mother stayed with her father, enduring his abuse for years. Miriam's parents eventually divorced when she was nine. "The women I knew had no power. I vowed never to let that happen to me," she recalled. Miriam promised herself that she would never back down from a challenge, no matter what obstacles stood in her way.

The Chicago Public Schools opened doors for her. In elementary school, several teachers recognized Miriam's intellect and promise. Her second-grade teacher told her parents she was gifted and got her into a private school, but that opportunity didn't pan out. Eventually, another teacher connected Miriam with A Better Chance, a nonprofit that placed talented children of color in private schools. Its alumni include-Deval Patrick, former governor of Massachusetts, and notable singer and songwriter Tracy Chapman.[4] Miriam applied to the program, and when she went to the recruiting event at the Park Hyatt Chicago, she realized she didn't know anyone who had stayed at the fancy downtown hotel. "The only people I knew who went to hotels like this were those who worked as cleaners," she recalled.

Miriam went on to earn a place at the selective and expensive Phillips Exeter Academy. She and a couple of dozen low-income inner-city teens of color moved from big cities to a town of ten thousand people in the middle of New Hampshire, where their classmates were mostly white and from upper-class families. Even today, the town is over 95 percent white, and Miriam was struck by a sense of dislocation and confusion about being so far from everything she knew.[5] She quietly watched as half her classmates of color dropped out, largely because of the cultural divide; they had moved from homes where they had little to a place where they were surrounded by affluence. But Miriam pushed through her first year there, realizing after earning grades that gave her high honors that she was as good a student as her classmates.

After two years Miriam decided to leave the school on her own terms and return to Chicago. There she enrolled at the Latin School of Chicago, which was closer to home and felt more culturally accessible. This experience taught her the importance of owning her path and pursuing what she needed. She carried this lesson with her for the rest of her career.

Each time Miriam saw a closed door, she figured out a way to go around it. An avid researcher and reader, she applied to Stanford and attended on scholarship and work-study. To make ends meet, she worked in the career center, connecting students with jobs. There she witnessed the power of technology and what it could accomplish, and she wanted to do more. Unsure of whether to get her law or business degree, Miriam did both, earning a JD and an MBA.

Miriam went on to found a startup with her new husband, Clint Korver, and soon had her first child. They were able to raise their angel and a Series A round of funding. When they reached Series B, however, the VCs refused to fund them if Miriam stayed. As she was fired, one of the board members said to her, "If you were my daughter, I would want you to stay home with my grandchild."

Miriam was undaunted by this setback, and she sought a new path. She wrote a letter to Gabriel Sandoval, a prominent Mexican American attorney who worked at Ariba, and talked her way through the switchboard to secure a meeting with him. At that lunch, he made her a job offer, and she accepted on the spot. Later, when Ariba were laying off attorneys, Miriam asked for the severance package and joined a startup called Google to work as their second lawyer. There she rose to the rank of vice president / deputy general counsel.

At a critical juncture in her career, Miriam could have pursued a path to general counsel or a vice president of strategy role at Google. Instead, she took a step back and decided to keep exploring. Seeing the inequity of the venture capital landscape, she decided to raise her own fund and create Ulu Ventures. Ulu is dedicated to funding diverse founder teams who are overlooked and less likely to get support. More than three quarters of its investments went to startups led by women, minority, or immigrant founders, well above the industry average.[6] To date, the firm has over $200 million under management and has funded ten companies that reached a valuation of over $1 billion, also known as unicorns. Three of them are now public: SoFi, Palantir, and Proterra.

Miriam's success wasn't inevitable. Many of those who grew up around her could not escape their upbringing. Instead, they struggled with addiction, poverty, and homelessness. But Miriam never let any challenges stand in her way, and she actively carved her path forward. She clung to these words: "With God all things are possible" (Matthew 19:26). Time after time, she could have allowed her circumstances to crush her, but each time, she chose not to let them win. While she wouldn't have been blamed for taking a free pass and giving up, she instead persevered, creating opportunities where none appeared to exist.

Learning to Ask

Dr. Ellen Ochoa ended her career as the center director of the Johnson Space Center, the first Hispanic and second woman to hold that position. Earlier in her career, she was two rungs below the top, reporting to an organizational director who in turn reported to the center director. The center director asked for her advice about a candidate for her manager's role. She gave her opinion on the candidate and then said, "I hope I would also be considered a strong candidate for the position when the time comes."

He responded, "Oh, you would be interested in moving up to director?"

Ellen recounted her reaction. "I realized that, like many women, I assumed that my accomplishments and hard work spoke for themselves. I hadn't actually expressed my career desires to either my supervisor or the center director, and it was obvious that other candidates, who were all male, had."

Had Ellen not spoken up, she might have ended up working for one of her peers instead of eventually becoming the second woman to hold the top job at the Johnson Space Center. She could have sat back and wondered why she was never considered. Instead, she asked, knowing the answer could have been negative. She took the shot, got the job, and then the next one after that, all because she learned to ask.

How many times have we not asked for what we wanted and then wondered why we didn't get it? Ironically, sometimes others are waiting for us to raise our hands. If we give ourselves a free pass, perhaps they will decide we don't really want it or that we aren't ready, forcing us to report to a peer or train our own manager.

This is what happened to Maeley Tom, one of the most influential Asian American women in California politics. During her tenure from 1974 to 1994—a time when few women and minorities played a role in the upper echelons of political circles—Maeley Tom was a pioneer. For seven years Maeley served on the administrative staff of Speaker Willie Brown Jr. as the deputy to the chief administrative officer (CAO). During this time, Maeley hired and trained a new CAO as her boss to support Brown as his right hand in the California State Assembly. This was the highest nonelected staff position in the chamber. When the first CAO left, Maeley hired and trained a second one. When he later departed, she hired and trained a third. After three CAOs came and went, she approached the legendary speaker of the assembly and said, "If I am good enough to train three CAOs, I should be good enough to be the CAO."

Brown paused for a long moment and replied, "Maeley, what took you so long to ask?"

Maeley dutifully and faithfully served Brown by hiring and training her bosses, but she never raised her hand on her own behalf. Over and over she handed her power to someone else, allowing others to take the reins until she spoke up. The minute she did, Brown deemed her ready for the role. After serving as the CAO of the Assembly, she broke another glass ceiling in the California legislature by becoming the first minority woman to serve as the chief of staff to the president of the California Senate before departing for a successful career in the private sector.[7]

Looking back, Maeley recalled, "I could not find a reason why I was not capable of performing all the duties of the top position, because I was training my own bosses. This [was] what finally made me realize that if I believed I could do it, then it was up to me—and no one else—to take the risk and ask for the job."

How many women quietly train their own bosses before they realize it is time to speak up?

Asking means taking a risk that you will hear the answer "no." Putting yourself out there means that sometimes you will fail to get what you want when you want it. But if you aren't hearing no on a regular basis, you aren't asking enough. As Carol Isozaki highlights to those she coaches, "A free pass is not free. There's a huge cost." Each time you don't speak up, each time you sit back and don't speak up, each time you don't ask for that opportunity, you pay a price. It is invisible but ever-present.

The price for not putting yourself out there is not having influence, not being invited to the next meeting, not getting that promotion. A vast majority of women who ask for raises don't receive them, but that's no reason not to try. You will get what you want only if you learn to actively seek it. As Ellen's and Maeley's experiences show, not speaking up has a cost, one that may be much higher than you can possibly imagine.

Tear up your free pass and take back your power.

Chart Your
Own Course

*Most people overestimate what they can do in one
year and underestimate what they can do in ten
years.*

—MODERN MAXIM

When I was little, my parents were honest with me about their expectations for our lives. As immigrants, they wanted us to have a life with stability and ease. I remember asking them how they felt about living in a tidy subdivision in a small town in the South. My dad replied that this type of peace was what he had dreamed of his whole life. I didn't get it. We lived in a small town where people treated us terribly, but this didn't bother him. How could this be the American dream?

My parents were born to large families. My father had seven living brothers and sisters, and my mother had six. Though they were middle class growing up in Vietnam, there was little food to go around. Eventually, they fled Vietnam and went to Hong Kong. They subsequently made their way to America individually for college. Though their families knew each other and they lived only a few blocks apart in Vietnam, they did not meet until they were in their late twenties in New York City.

Later in his life, when my father was diagnosed with stage IV cancer and given less than a year to live, he said he was content with the life he had lived. I didn't understand. But having fled Vietnam to go to Hong Kong, and then traveling from Hong Kong to America alone, he had seen hardship unlike anything I had known. He told me of a time when his family was so poor, they ate only rice and vegetables and rarely had access to meat. Because he was so sickly as a child, his nursemaid hid extra protein under my father's rice, but his siblings went without. When he came to America with little to nothing, he could barely afford to eat and resorted to mixing milk with rice for dinner. He never let us waste a grain of rice without reminding us how lucky we were to never have to worry about food.

My father's workplace discriminated against him, not granting him the title and compensation of an electrical engineer even though he held a degree and instead keeping him as a technician. This discrimination was what prompted our move from New York to South Carolina, a state my parents had barely even heard of, let alone visited.

I hated growing up in a place where I was forever marked by being different, but to my parents, this was the American dream. They wanted and expected my sister and me to live the life that was set before us: Study hard. Do well in school. Get a scholarship to a good college. Find a suitable job. Marry well. Have 2.5 children and live in a house with a white picket fence in a neat suburb with a trim lawn and maybe a dog.

I was a striver, an achiever. Put a goal in front of me, and I worked toward it. When I was in the third grade, my teacher once dropped a list on the ground. It wasn't in alphabetical order, so I convinced myself it was a class ranking. My name showed up fifth. I decided then and there that I would graduate as the valedictorian of my high school class. Nine years later, I did. I applied to college knowing my parents didn't have the money to support both my sister and me at the same time, so I feverishly applied for scholarships. A scholarship to Duke and funding from a dozen other groups covered much of my tuition. Later, when I got my first job, I showed my father the offer. He laughed and said proudly, "You make more as a brand-new graduate than I make now after nearly thirty years as an engineer."

But it was never enough. I always felt like I had something to prove. I knew I wanted to go to graduate school, so on a whim, I applied to law school. Shockingly, I was accepted into Yale, but my then-boyfriend, who was at Harvard Law School at the time, convinced me I would hate law school and that I should apply to business school instead. So I spent a couple of years at Boston Consulting Group and set my sights on Stanford for my MBA.

After Stanford, I took a job at PayPal and then eBay and then Facebook. The day I joined Facebook, they showed me a picture of the "M-Team," the small group of people who led the company. I vowed that I would get there someday. Five years later, I did.

But then what? A house, a mortgage, and a simple life. Build one more product, get one more promotion, climb one rung further up this invisible ladder. One day I woke up and asked myself, "Is this all there is?"

The ladder is infinite if you are willing to climb it, and there is never a top rung. The reward for climbing higher is seeing what you haven't yet accomplished. But what I didn't realize then was that someone else had constructed the ladder, and I was living by their definition of success, not mine. Once I learned that I could forge my own path, I realized how much power I truly held.

Pursue Your Dream

Abigail Wen created a successful career in artificial intelligence at Intel. Secretly, she also wrote for an hour or two each night—for twelve years. By day, she led an AI business development and investments practice within her company. By night, she dreamed of telling the stories that reflected her background as an Asian American woman coming of age in Ohio.

Like many children of immigrants, Abigail had a clear career path early on. She attended Harvard University as an undergraduate, then Columbia Law School, where she earned her JD. She checked all the boxes to become a law professor in academia: editing the *Columbia Law Review*, clerking for the US Court of Appeals for the DC Circuit, and practicing at a well-respected law firm. Then, when the time came, she realized that her dream was to write fiction for young adults.

So she pivoted. Moving out to Silicon Valley, she joined Intel to lead their AI efforts and built a reputation as "one of the most respected voices on fairness in AI."[1] During this long stretch of time, Abigail also wrote four novels, none of which were picked up by publishing houses. Despite repeated rejections, Abigail kept writing.

Then came *Loveboat, Taipei*. This book was a fictional version of her experience as a high school student spending the summer in Taiwan, away from home for the first time. She sent it to an agent, who took it into a bidding war, landing her a six-figure contract and a multibook deal. It launched as a *New York Times* bestseller, which led Abigail to a whole new path beyond Intel. She teamed up with the producers of the Netflix hit franchise *To All the Boys I've Loved Before* to turn *Loveboat, Taipei* into a film before leaving her corporate job to produce and write full-time. She ended up launching a production company and bringing other stories of Asian Americans to life on the screen.

Abigail decided to chart her own course, not the one preordained for her, and she worked for it even when achieving it didn't seem possible. She hosted a podcast on artificial intelligence and turned her book into a movie. She published a sequel, *Loveboat Reunion*; her first short story, "The Idiom Algorithm"; and her first graphic novel, *The Fidget Booth* (forthcoming). She signed on with a legendary film manager and is now creating original TV series and films about themes she has been passionate about her whole life: family, culture, ethics, tech, leadership, and international relations.

By pursuing her dream of becoming a writer, Abigail opened a door to a world she knew little about. Though her days were filled with her expertise in AI, her nights were filled with writing, editing, and publishing. Rather than give up her dream, she secretly nurtured it and honed her skills. She jokes that she may seem like an overnight success, but her success was more than ten years in the making. She never let her dream die, even when she faced the harsh reality of rejection.

Nearly everyone has a dream, but it remains a dream if you don't make progress toward it. Every night when Abigail wrote, she was one day closer to becoming a bestselling author, even though it was more than a decade away. Along the way, she honed her craft, met with other writers, and earned a master's of fine arts from the Vermont College of Fine Arts.

If you have a dream, start by doing a little bit each day. Whether it is learning a language so you can work abroad, working on an idea for a new business, or investing in new skills to level up your career, set aside a small amount of time each day to get you closer to where you want to go. An idea can turn into a hobby, a hobby can turn into your vocation, and a vocation can turn into your career. We tend to want immediate results and become discouraged if we can't achieve them, but over time, we can bend the future. It all starts with a plan and the willingness to put in the time to see it through.

I started writing this book a little at a time. For years I wrote and published articles internally at work. That slowly evolved to publishing in mainstream news outlets, including *Forbes*, *Quartz*, and *Entrepreneur*. Each evening, I spent at least thirty minutes writing something. Most of that writing remains confined to my computer, but it taught me the discipline of getting words on the blank screen. Each time I wrote, I worried that no one would want to read it, but eventually, I decided I would write for the one person who needed to read it that day, rather than trying to please everyone.

I learned slowly to share my story, one essay at a time, and eventually, I compiled those into what became this book.

If you have an aspiration, start by breaking it down.

- Write down your goal with a two-year to five-year time horizon.
- Break down your goal into tangible and achievable units with monthly or quarterly milestones.
- Set a specific amount of time each day to invest in this project.
- Seek accountability through a friend or a group, and set weekly milestones for checking in with them.
- Allow yourself space for setbacks and detours.

A goal map is a great place to start, no matter what your dream is. In the center, write what you want to achieve in two to five years. Then, around the central goal, break down three to five subgoals you need to do to achieve your goal. In the outer circles, write out the three to five things you need to do to meet the subgoals. Place this goal map in a prominent place where you will see it. Here is a sample goal map:

In a 2015 study by Dr. Gail Matthews, those who simply wrote down their goals were 33 percent more likely to achieve them.[2] But those who wrote down their goals and also shared their weekly progress with a friend had even greater success. Abigail went to a writing circle with a small group of friends. Over those twelve years, they swapped work, gave one another feedback, and helped each other find success. Each of the women in Abigail's group was published except for her, but their encouragement helped her continue to write through the years when there seemed to be no end in sight.

Charting your own course isn't easy, but breaking down the problem and seeking support and accountability can be the secret to long-term success.

Turn Stumbling Blocks into Stepping-Stones

Sanyin Siang long called herself "the girl with a plan." She graduated as the valedictorian of her high school and won the prestigious A. B. Duke Scholarship, which Duke University awards to only the top few applicants each year.

From a young age, Sanyin wanted to be a doctor, and she worked toward that goal her whole life. During her junior year in college, because of her slipping grades, she lost her scholarship, and her dreams of becoming a doctor disappeared overnight. While her future had once been clear, she now faced a yawning void. Her disappointment in herself over the loss of her dream devastated her.

So "the girl with a plan" now had to come up with a new one. Sanyin turned that failure into the catalyst to write her next chapter. Now free to explore all her options for the first time, Sanyin regrouped and decided to explore a different path. This eventually led her back to Duke to get her executive MBA from the Fuqua School of Business. She then founded and became executive director of the Fuqua/Coach K Center on Leadership and Ethics, a role she has held for nearly two decades.

Today Sanyin coaches CEOs, well-known athletes, and military leaders. She has over a million followers on LinkedIn who learn from her experience. She sits on the board of multiple companies and nonprofits. This was all possible because of that stumbling block when she was twenty-one, which became her stepping-stone to success.

We all fail at one point or another. The only decision we can make is whether to let that failure define us. When I was in business school, I wanted to work abroad during the summer between my first and second years. I took an internship at McKinsey & Company in Hong Kong, which allowed me to live out my dream of spending time with my grandmother and explore working abroad. But at the end of that summer, I didn't receive an offer to return to McKinsey full-time. To not be invited back to a prestigious firm after a summer internship signaled failure and was deeply crushing. I haven't talked about it until now. Looking back, I realize now that it was also the reason I didn't fall back to the safety of consulting and instead took a risk joining a startup, PayPal, in Silicon Valley. This opened the door to the rest of my career.

Career paths are not linear. They don't always go up and to the right. When we encounter failures or obstacles, we can allow them to knock us down or use them as catalysts to grow stronger and seek a different way around. Even if your ultimate goal is no longer possible, your detour may take you to wonderful and unexpected places. In many ways, the greatest failure in Sanyin's life turned into the best thing that ever happened to her. She allowed herself to trade her original dream for a new one. Rather than giving in to despair, she found freedom.

Setbacks and frustrations are inevitable. There will be moments when you feel you have reached a dead end, when just on the other side of the next hill is a new opportunity. I interviewed over two dozen women for this book, and despite the success they each achieved, every single one faced significant challenges. What they all had in common was their resilience, their ability to look beyond failure and build a new future for themselves.

Many women get stuck on their first failure, but rather than letting your first "no" turn into the end of the road, see it as the beginning of something new. The moment you hit the wall may be the impetus you need to change direction. Turn it into the jumping-off point to create an even better future.

Katia Verresen is known as the "Tech Exec Whisperer." She is a prominent executive coach in Silicon Valley, and her practice has helped shape the people who build products that much of the world uses. But this career was not her original plan.

Born in France, Katia had roots in many cultures. Her maternal grandfather was Chinese, and her maternal grandmother was Scottish-Canadian. Her paternal grandfather was French-Belgian, and her paternal grandmother was Italian. Many of them left their homes, and even their countries, to seek out opportunities in new places and reinvent themselves. At sixteen, Katia followed in their footsteps, leaving France for America. There, she put herself on the path to becoming a lawyer. After interning at the most prominent law firm in Silicon Valley, she felt her career was in motion.

Just after she graduated, Katia was rear-ended in a terrible car accident. This led to over a year of physical therapy and a struggle with her new profession due to her inability to sit for more than a short period. Being a lawyer meant working in front of a computer for hours, and this setback forced her to rethink her plans. Katia realized she couldn't continue on her current path and heal her body at the same time.

This realization led her back to Europe, where she joined the well-known investor and venture capitalist Guy Kawasaki to build out his investment marketplace. There she learned the ins and outs of technology investing and settled into a job that she loved in a space she enjoyed. That all changed once more after September 11, 2001, when the whole world was shaken. Katia was laid off and without a backup plan.

Deciding to reinvent herself again, Katia started her own coaching firm. She decided to coach her own way, not through formulas or to-do lists but by understanding the deep wounds that hold people back and helping to heal them, allowing them to move forward. Katia went on to coach founders, executives, and investors across startups and large tech companies. Her services are in such high demand that she takes new clients only by referrals and keeps a months-long waiting list. She told me the first time she met me that I would be CEO someday, and I laughed at her suggestion. Now, looking back a decade later, I know it was her wisdom and encouragement that got me to where I am today.

Though she did not plan to, Katia charted her own course and redefined what success looks like for both herself and her clients. If it weren't for that car accident, she would never have ended up at Guy's firm. If she hadn't been laid off, she wouldn't have become the coach, writer, and podcaster that she is today. If it weren't for the pandemic, she would not have scaled up her one-on-one coaching to create a new Foundations of Inner Power class that has touched thousands of executives. Each stumbling block in her life could have stopped her. Instead, they brought out Katia's inner resilience and drove her to seek out something new. These challenges were the push she needed to pivot and reinvent herself, and they led her to help others find that same strength in themselves. Katia lives each day by her mantra: "We can't control everything that happens to us, but we are born creators and can create possibilities from anything."

In 2019 two professors from the Kellogg School of Management, Dashun Wang and Benjamin Jones, published a study of more than one thousand junior scientists who applied for a grant from the US National Institutes of Health between 1990 and 2005.[3] They focused on scientists who were just above and below the cutoff where funding was granted. Unsurprisingly, those who missed getting that specific grant had a 10 percent higher probability of leaving academic research, but for those who stayed, something unexpected happened. Those who persisted, despite not receiving the grant, ended up having as much impact as those who received it—if not more.

If I had gotten an offer at McKinsey & Company during business school, I would likely have taken it and missed out on the chance to explore a career in the technology field. While failure is often seen as a negative, it can be leveraged as the springboard toward something new, an opportunity to try something you've previously left unexplored.

For every "no," there is an opportunity for a different "yes." That "yes" may be something you never considered. Three times during my career at Facebook, the CEO, Mark Zuckerberg, asked me to give up large portions of my team to other parts of the business. Each time I was devastated. I had built many of the products and teams from scratch, and being asked to hand them over to other leaders felt like being told I was failing. I was angry that he would ask this of me when I had put my heart and soul into them. Each time I contemplated leaving the company.

In the workplace, we often equate scope with career advancement. Owning more means being more important or impactful. But sometimes the opposite is true. Doing too many things means giving too little attention to any single thing, which creates a struggle to keep up with disparate areas that don't align.

I couldn't see that, but Mark did. He asked me to give away Facebook platform, including Facebook Analytics, Games, the Audience Network, and App Install Ads to multiple other teams. I loved the products, the people, and the communities we served. My role had become a big part of my identity. The ability to reach over a billion people through more than a million apps allowed us to be more than a great product; it allowed us to be an enabler of many other great products. The chief marketing officer of a company that would later be sold for nearly $2 billion told me they existed only because of the impact of our developer platform, especially App Ads, which helped them scale at a time when they were almost shut down. I recently learned of a developer in India who leverages our tools to connect moms who would otherwise not have a community to rely on, especially where their access to the internet is extremely limited.

But none of this impact changed the fact that the worlds of Facebook platform and Facebook commerce were pulling apart, and the moment came for me to let my previous work go in order to nurture my next product. I remember the day I was told about the reorganization and how the work of over 150 people would be moving into five organizations. I barely ate and slept for those three weeks as we figured out how to execute it. I struggled with how to say goodbye to teams, people, and products I loved and had invested so much in.

I saw this shift as a major career failure, a sign that I wasn't good enough. I felt angry, even at times betrayed, that what I accomplished wasn't enough, that I didn't prove my worth. But six months later, I realized that by closing that door, Mark had forced me to focus my attention on something new. I had already started to slowly build what would later become Facebook Marketplace. Over the next several years, we built it into one of the most widely used websites in the world, supporting millions of sellers and over a billion visitors each month. That wouldn't have happened if Mark had not cut me off from my other distractions.

During times of turbulence and uncertainty, it is easy to feel defeated. When you are overlooked for the promotion, when your idea is shot down by your boss, or when you are passed over for the project you wanted to work on, allow yourself to mourn. Give your-self space and a specific timeline to process, then come up with a new plan. The best way to avoid getting seasick is to look toward the horizon and seek what lies ahead.

Look for Step Functions

Throughout childhood, our paths are linear. Preschool to elementary school. Middle school to high school. Perhaps college, which then leads into the workforce. The path is well-worn, and the expectations are clear. But when you enter the workplace, what made you successful in the fixed lanes of school are often what will cause you to stumble. There are no tests, no study guides to keep you on track.

Often, life outside of school bewilders the best students because the possibilities are endless, and the paths diverge in many ways. No longer able to measure success by semesters, grades, class rank, and graduation, those who thrived on the regimented path must find new ways to adapt. By learning to seek out and embrace the nonlinear path, we can propel ourselves to new heights.

Peggy Alford is a prominent leader in Silicon Valley, being both the executive vice president of global sales at PayPal and a member of the Facebook board. Peggy grew up in St. Louis, Missouri, as one of six adopted, multiethnic children. Her mother, Mary Abkemeier, was a pioneer, one of the few women of her time to hold a PhD in math and computer science, serving as a professor of math, computer science, and cybersecurity, which was nearly unheard of during that era. Though Peggy aspired to attend law school, she changed her major to accounting to ensure that she could land a job and support herself and her family.

As a Black, Latina, and White mixed-race woman working in

St. Louis and Baltimore, Peggy joined a premier accounting firm, serving clients in education, government, and health care, areas that didn't spark her interest. She recalled, "Women and people of color weren't getting the good assignments. They were pigeonholed into 'safe' industries, whereas the technical, high-profile, and coveted client engagements went to others." When given the opportunity to take a one-year assignment at the firm's Silicon Valley office during the boom of the late 1990s, she jumped at the chance to carve a different path for herself. When it came time to return to her home office, Peggy asked a partner if she would return to doing the "women friendly" areas she had worked in before.

He said, "Yes."

In response, Peggy took back her power by negotiating a way to stay at the Silicon Valley office. She said to herself, "I am not going to put myself back into a position where I don't get to choose my path. I'm not going back."

Eventually, she made her way to eBay, where she rose through the ranks in finance. Then she took an unusual assignment for a woman: Peggy went to Los Angeles and became the chief financial officer (CFO) for a subsidiary, Rent.com. When the president departed, she saw a chance to take on the role, but Peggy was never once promoted and remained a senior director, despite running the entire business. "Don't focus on the next promotion," she advises. "Instead, focus on broadening your skills so that the next opportunity can be four rungs up the ladder."

Peggy focused on growing her career through step functions, opportunities to build skills that would allow her to leapfrog past those who took the linear path. She went from one major step to another, from eBay to PayPal to the Chan Zuckerberg Initiative, where she served as the CFO and head of operations. She then returned to PayPal to lead global sales and became a part of their executive team.

When Peggy left Chan Zuckerberg, Mark Zuckerberg asked her to join the board of Facebook. She replied, "You do realize I will be the least successful person on the board, right?" Mark disagreed and persuaded her to take the role.

Peggy initially felt out of her depth advising one of the most influential companies in the world. But since then she has built a closer personal relationship with Mark, becoming a powerful voice on the board during a tumultuous time in the company's history.

Peggy never focused on climbing the ladder designed by someone else; instead, she defied expectations and charted her own course. Each step she took taught her skills that would open doors she could once only dream of.

Carve Your Own Path

Carving your path often means taking a road that others didn't travel first. This road is risky and unclear, but it is also yours to create. Success is no longer defined by climbing an organizational chart or seeking the next promotion; rather, it is crafting something unique and new.

Sapna Cheryan is a professor at the University of Washington, where she leads the Stereotypes, Identity, and Belonging Lab. She is a pioneer in research on gender stereotypes and the barriers to women entering science, technology, engineering, and math (STEM) fields. Her insights into why girls are attracted to STEM and what pushes them away from the field have changed the face of many college programs and influenced recruiting throughout the tech industry. In 2014 President Barack Obama awarded her a prize for her classroom design to encourage more women to enter the field.[4]

Sapna's journey toward this work started in high school when she and her classmates all enrolled in mandatory computer science classes. She recounts, "Breakthroughs were attributed largely to young, white men. The broader image of who the computer geniuses were looked nothing like the girls in my high school." Though she and many of her female friends earned As in the class, none of them went on to make computer science a career. Instead, they became academics, business leaders, and doctors. This was a marked contrast to many of her male classmates, who went on to study computer science and enter the technology field.

She puzzled through why there was such a pronounced gender difference. During college, she interviewed for an internship in user research at two technology firms. The first exemplified stereotypical "geek culture," with conference rooms named after *Star Trek* ships. The second was Adobe, with a more colorful yet neutral design. Sapna chose the latter, even though it was a longer commute and lower pay.

Her high school and college experiences led her to ask what in the field of technology attracted women to or turned women away from the path. One of her key papers, funded by the National Science Foundation, pointed to a geek-oriented and masculine environment that could turn women off from the pursuit of STEM.[5] She had students enter a computer science room—one with *Star Trek* posters and video game motifs and the other with neutral posters and decorations—and asked them afterward about their interest in studying computer science. While men showed no difference in desire, women who were shown the geeky room were much less likely to want to study computer science. Women, on average, also signaled a preference for the neutral room.

Sapna went on to study how stereotypes of the prototypical geek—unwashed, pale, awkward, and into science fiction and video games—discouraged women from entering the field but had less impact on driving men away. Women responded to their discomfort with these images by rejecting computer science as a field of study. When Sapna showed these students an article about computer scientists that contradicted these negative stereotypes, she made a major impact in their desire to enter the field.[6]

By unpacking her journey from high school to college to academia, Sapna sought to understand the path that had led her away from STEM. Her research changed the way we talk about STEM culture and impacted hundreds of campuses and companies. While she didn't end up in the field, she transformed it for tens of thousands of women who can now experience belonging in a new way.

No one gave Sapna a road map to her career and field of research. She took her experiences and skills and crafted one of her own. Sometimes the path you seek is one that has not yet been traveled. It may require you to plow new ground and craft a new way forward. You become a pioneer, traversing unknown and unmapped territories. The journey is uniquely yours.

Remember that your path is not set. Your fate is not sealed, and you always have a new chance to move toward your goal. Life is not just about the big moments. Rather, it is a game of inches in which you take a small step every day toward your goal.

Women like Abigail, Sanyin, Peggy, Katia, and Sapna didn't follow someone else's road map and instead made their journeys their own.

As you write your life story, decide which set paths you want to take and which detours and adventures you want to pursue. You may not follow a straight line or go straight up a corporate ladder, but being willing to take risks and chart your own course means you can succeed on your own terms.

Build a Learning
Mindset

It doesn't matter how you got there. It matters what
you do now that you're there.

—CHRISTINE TSAI

We are taught in school to seek "mastery": the ability to understand something so well that we can teach it to others. We spend years striving to attain it. We measure ourselves through grades, class rank, honor rolls, awards, and standardized test scores—all with the goal of mastery. We learn to focus on getting the right answer, getting the highest test score, achieving the A.

Then we get into the workforce, and we are fish out of water. The people around us bring different experiences. Some are more strategic, while others are stronger executors. Some people seem to know exactly what to say when put on the spot, while we watch every word, worried that we are getting it wrong. We hear people pitching their ideas and selling their narratives, and we wonder where they learned how to do that. These intangible skills no one taught us in the classroom suddenly become more important than the actual work product. We wonder whether we will ever measure up. Everyone seems smarter, more sophisticated, and better suited for the job. We look around and wonder if we somehow made a mistake.

Imposter syndrome happens when there is no grade to prove to you that you are good enough and no test to demonstrate your expertise. You sit there, worried that you were let in accidentally and that someone will inevitably find you out.

This feeling is even more acute when you are "the only," someone who doesn't look like everyone else. You feel singled out. You are not only being judged on your merits but also feel the weight of being different. It weighs heavy on you.

I am regularly asked how often I feel like an impostor.

"Every single day" is always my response.

A 2020 KPMG study of women executives found that 75 percent of them experienced imposter syndrome at some point in their careers, and 85 percent considered it a normal occurrence in corporate life.[1] These numbers illustrate the universality of the problem: it's the secret that no one wants to say out loud, like in *The Emperor's New Clothes*. We constantly worry that people will realize we have no idea what we're doing. But there's a flip side. If a vast majority of those around us feel this way, then that means we are in this together. We are all far more capable than we give ourselves credit for. By embracing our adaptability and ability to learn, we can succeed in ways we never could have imagined.

Fake It Until You Make It

Throughout my career, I have taken on many roles even though I was barely qualified to do the work. I stumbled into the tech field, having no idea what I was getting into. In 2002 I was about to graduate from Stanford Graduate School of Business (GSB) when I stopped by a campus career fair. I saw a table for a small company called PayPal, and as an avid eBay seller (eBay was part of PayPal at the time), I stopped by to tell them how much I loved their product. Tim Wenzel, the first recruiter at PayPal, and Katherine Woo, a recent GSB alumna, were staffing the booth. After chatting for a few minutes, they asked me to come to their office the next day for an interview. I was planning to move back to North Carolina, but I accepted the meeting because I was curious what their office was like. Tim told me, "We have openings in product and in marketing. Which do you prefer?"

I had taken some marketing classes, but I had no idea what a product manager did. So I turned to Katherine and asked her, "What do you do?"

She replied, "I work in product."

I said, "Sounds good."

That spur-of-the-moment decision had lasting consequences. The truth was, I didn't know what it meant to work in "product." Since I did not intend to take the job, I decided to wing the interviews and hope no one noticed. Then I could tell my friends back home in North Carolina about my brush with a hot Silicon Valley startup.

For two days I met groups of people who asked me questions about what I would want as an eBay seller. I eagerly shared my ideas, while at the same time desperately trying to get them to tell me what the role was. After the interviews, my husband and I sat down and talked seriously about whether we wanted to move back south when the economy was still in tatters. We decided to stay for a year or two to ride out the recession, and I took the job at PayPal.

When I arrived on my first day, I knew that the jig was up. I went to Amy Klement, the vice president of product management, my new skip-level manager. I told her I had no idea what the role entailed but that I would learn everything she had to teach me. Graciously, she sat down and patiently explained every element of the role. Rather than treat me as an imposter, she saw my trepidation, embraced me, and taught me how to do the job. Her allyship during this critical time gave me the confidence to learn the skills.

Less than two weeks later, PayPal announced it had been acquired by eBay, and Amy entrusted me to lead the product integration from the PayPal side. When my manager left not long after, Amy interviewed several senior candidates and ended up deciding to offer me the opportunity to manage the product and team for our largest line of business: eBay. She took a chance on me when I was only twenty-six to do something I had no experience doing. I walked in every day feeling like an imposter, wondering when she would figure out that she had made a terrible mistake and replace me with someone qualified to do the job. So I did the only thing I knew how: I rolled up my sleeves and got to work hiring and growing the people on the team. I knew I wasn't the most experienced, but I could work hard and learn fast to compensate for what I lacked.

Years later I went out to lunch with a group of senior PayPal product leaders, and we joked that we joined when we were so green that none of us would even qualify to interview for our own teams today. That experience taught me something important: that a learning mindset trumps expertise every time.

Learning to Learn

The most important skill I have learned is how to continue to learn. There have been many times when I asked someone to step up to manage a team, and they responded that they couldn't do it. When I asked why, they would reply, "How can I teach someone if I'm not better than them at the job?" But think about CEOs. How many of them are better than their CFO at finance or their general counsel at understanding the law?

During the time I was working on app ads, my new manager, Doug Purdy, said to me, "To be a successful PM on the platform team, you will need to be able to code. That is the only way to build empathy with developers."

I had not coded since college, and I didn't major in computer science, so I replied, "I will probably be the worst PM on your team, then." A couple of years later, when Doug left the team, he recommended me as his successor despite my lack of coding skills. Eventually, I took over the whole product team, and a year later, I took over his manager's job running both our team and engineering.

I was leading the platform team. In the back of my mind, I wondered if I was truly qualified to do so. But not knowing much about developers was freeing because I had no preconceived notions about what they wanted or needed. It also taught me to be curious and to listen to their needs. It turns out that stability and predictability mattered more than new features and exciting launches, and we spent the next several years ensuring we were meeting those needs. Over several years we grew our net promoter score, the ratings that developers gave our platform, from net negative to positive.

What I brought to the table was not expertise, but rather fresh eyes and a willingness to reexamine the problem from the beginning. Rather than trust my judgment, I listened, learned, and iterated. I sought answers through questions, not through personal experience, and that meant I led differently.

Be Open to Opportunities

I have worked on many products in industries I didn't understand. I knew those types of opportunities could paralyze me or be an opportunity to look at the problem differently. My career at Facebook is an example of this: I was a casual Facebook user, and I didn't know much about it beyond posting to my friends. But I became more and more excited as I read about the potential of what Facebook could become. In 2009 I interviewed for a role called product marketing for consumer monetization, and I joined, not sure what that entailed. Part of the adventure of Facebook is that you can define your work based on what you choose to spend your time on, and it's that flexibility and self-organization that makes it possible for us to move fast and have an impact. I worked on the Facebook Gift Shop, Games, and the original Marketplace, and eventually, we launched Facebook Credits.

When I returned from maternity leave, I was asked to work on mobile monetization. My background was in commerce and payments, and I had never worked on mobile or ads. Eventually, after speaking to many game developers I knew from my days on Games and Credits, we decided to build in mobile app ads, an industry we knew nothing about.

We iterated on the idea over several months through mostly trial and error and customer feedback. I didn't internalize how little we knew until one of our game developers, who were advertising partners, called me and shared, "Wow, this product is great. You are sending us real customers."

I laughed and said, "What other kinds are there?" I immediately called a friend who had worked in the industry to ask what that partner had meant. He explained charting, bot farms, and how students in Asia are paid to download and install apps. Not having the baggage of worrying about what the rest of the industry was doing freed our mobile app ads team to do what no one had focused on before: building a platform for app discovery and a people-centric model of app advertising.

Today this business accounts for billions of dollars of company revenues and continues to lead in the space, and it's all because we focused on what was possible, regardless of how the industry was working at the time.

Beginner's Mind

There is freedom in not being the expert and instead focusing on being the student. Building great products is often less about the experience and more about the ability to test, learn, and pivot. Having a beginner's mind allows you to explore the problem in new ways and not be trapped in a fixed way of thinking.

Tom Wujec, an author and speaker on creativity, has given the marshmallow challenge to different groups, from kindergarteners to MBAs to C-suite executives. He gives a group of four a marshmallow, some string, tape, and twenty pieces of uncooked spaghetti. The goal is to build a self-sustaining structure to get the marshmallow as high as possible at the end of the eighteen-minute time limit.[2] Surprisingly, kindergarteners outperform everyone in the exercise.

Why would children outperform their better-educated and more mature competitors? The answer is simple: children aren't born with a preconceived notion about what a solution looks like. Instead, they test and iterate, often resulting in collapsed towers, along with giggles, until they find something that works. Believing you are an expert fools you into believing you know the answer already, and thus you are less likely to be open-minded and willing to try a new way.

I often wonder if someone will finally figure out that I have no idea what I'm doing. But I decided long ago that letting that feeling dictate my actions is counterproductive. Instead, I choose to reframe my mindset from one of *impostor* to one of *explorer* because that is one area where I can truly be an expert.

I have failed. A lot. Learning to succeed means learning from failure. Each time you fail, it is not a stumbling block; rather, it becomes raw material you can use to help you achieve.

Learning through Loss

I was passed over for my dream job at Facebook twice in one year. Each time, I wanted to transfer and take on a new opportunity that was open within the company, and each time, I was told no. I wanted these roles badly, and I threw my hat in the ring. But the company was looking for something different than what I could offer at the time. Each "no" was heartbreaking in many ways, but each time it happened, in the subsequent months, I ended up doing my very best work.

I knew there were two ways I could react to losing out on something I wanted: I could regret, or I could create. Since it wasn't likely those specific opportunities would come again, I decided to shape the job I did have into the one I wanted. I took more risks and was bolder in designing the future. By having nothing to lose, I was able to be more assertive and unrepentant in how I approached problems, and it resulted in two of the most important products I will ever work on: Facebook Marketplace and Facebook Pay.

Learning to lead through loss and finding a path forward are critical to taking back your power when circumstances take it away.

Christine Tsai knows what it means to take the reins through loss. Today she is the CEO and founding partner of 500 (formerly known as 500 Startups), an early-stage venture capital firm focused on investing in founders from all around the world and helping them scale their companies. The journey she took there occurred during the most difficult time in her career.

In 2010, after spending seven years at Google, Christine wanted to break into venture capital, where women make up less than 5 percent of the investors.[3] She connected with Dave McClure and decided to leave the safety of Google to cofound 500 with him. For seven years Christine worked alongside Dave, the charismatic CEO and public face of the company. She served as his partner, the quiet, steadying force behind the scenes. Their funds focused on seeding the next generation of technology companies, including Twilio, The RealReal, Talkdesk, Canva, and Credit Karma, making the firm well-known around the world.

I worked with Dave McClure at PayPal, and my husband and I invested in several of the 500 funds. I watched with interest as Dave and Christine built a powerhouse of an investment firm. Then, in 2017, the firm faced a crisis of confidence when Dave was accused of sexual harassment in an article published in the *New York Times*.[4] Dave subsequently wrote an apology explaining his actions, which he later deleted.[5] On that note, he abruptly handed over the reins of 500 to Christine, making her the new CEO.

Leading a firm like 500 after the public departure of the CEO and cofounder pushed Christine into a role she had not expected. This was at a time when the #MeToo movement had engulfed Silicon Valley. Reflecting years later, Christine said, "Being thrust into the leadership role so suddenly, I felt even more uncomfortable with power because I felt like I didn't deserve it."

Under the searing lights of press scrutiny, she had to lead the firm forward. "It was the most difficult period of my life and, even to this day, is still painful to talk about. Yet at the time, the thought of walking away was unthinkable to me." The questions and rumors surrounding Dave's departure and resignation spread. Rather than letting this crush her, Christine found strength in her sense of loyalty to those she led: the team within the company, her investors, and the portfolio of company founders. She learned to lead through adversity and grew into her own.

What Christine didn't expect after taking the reins was the sense of trauma around how she arrived in the leadership position. "While the scars are still present, I'm learning to embrace them as part of the person I am today," she says.

Though she felt like an imposter, Christine learned to fight through it and become the leader that her firm needed to start its next chapter. She went on to grow 500's committed capital from $390 million to more than $780 million (and over $1.8B in assets under management), launch seven new funds, recruit new seasoned executives and managing partners, and lead the growth of the global portfolio to forty-one unicorns and counting. In the years since she took the reins, Christine has learned to lead a firm based on her particular strengths in a male-dominated field.

Christine showed what it means to grow from loss and adversity and learned to lead her own way. Being thrust into the limelight with all the attendant questions and scrutiny could have crushed her, but she instead grew stronger and bolder—not despite her experience but because of it.

Rebuilding from Nothing

When I got back from maternity leave after my son, Jonathan, was born, I was directionless and not sure I wanted to work in tech anymore. My career wasn't going anywhere, and the lack of opportunity for growth at PayPal at the time frustrated me. The same happened when I came back from maternity leave with my second child, Bethany. I returned to eBay and stared down the barrel of more years spent working on the integration between eBay and PayPal, something I had done for seven years already.

Later, at Facebook, after the birth of my third child, Danielle, I returned to a new manager and had no real role anymore. These moments were the most frustrating in my career, but they were also the most important turning points. After Jonathan, I left my job leading the eBay product at PayPal to become a part of product strategy, which then led me to build the social commerce and charity verticals. This subsequently led me to eBay, which I left after Bethany's birth to join Facebook. After Danielle, I left the payments group and was asked to work on mobile monetization, which led to Project Neko, or Mobile App Install Ads.

Each time I left to have a child, I started from scratch again. The bewildering feeling of loss and restarting almost crushed me. I felt like I had failed in my career each time, but looking back, I know the sense of having nothing to lose gave me the impetus to push on and take on something new.

Starting from nothing also means having nothing to lose and everything to gain. Rather than being constrained by your circumstances or commitments, you get a chance to reset and build your career on your own terms. That is the heart of the story of Whitney Wolfe Herd, one of the most well-known builders in the world.

Whitney Wolfe Herd is a woman of firsts. In 2014 she founded a women-focused dating app, Bumble. In 2021, at age thirty-one, she became the youngest woman to take a company public. In doing so, she became the youngest self-made female billionaire.[6] But her journey to the height of entrepreneurial success in the online dating space started with a different app, Tinder, which she cofounded. Whitney popularized the fledgling app by going to college campuses to engage the co-ed community and bring on early users, leading to a meteoric rise in the app's popularity. But in 2014 she was stripped of her cofounder title and eventually pushed out of Tinder. She went on to sue the company for harassment. The suit was settled, and she regained her cofounder title while also being awarded a reported $1 million. Her cofounders soon left the company.[7]

Unsure of what was next, Whitney focused on her new idea of building a social network that women could use to connect with one another. Andrey Andreev, the CEO and founder of Badoo, a social dating app, reached out and asked her to reconsider the dating space, offering to back her in founding a new company. Whitney decided to go back into the world she had wanted to leave behind, but on her terms. She developed the idea of Bumble around the notion that only women can make the first move. Leveraging the product, she addressed the biggest complaints about online dating: rejection for men and unwanted messages for women. Most dating apps required men to reach out to many women, only to get low response rates, while women received a barrage of messages, including harassing ones. By turning that mechanic on its head, Whitney made an app that spread through word of mouth. Because women were attracted to the app, it also brought in men, building a different kind of dating community that now has over one hundred million active users worldwide.[8]

As Bumble gained traction in 2017, the Match Group, which incubated and owned Tinder, took notice. They offered Whitney $450 million for Bumble, then upped their offer to $1 billion a few months later.[9] But Whitney stood firm and focused on growing her company. When Match sued Bumble for patent infringement and copying Tinder's look and feel, Bumble sued Match back later that year, accusing it of attempting to diminish the value of Bumble. Despite the continued back and forth between the two companies, Whitney relentlessly focused on building the app and growing its engagement, now under Andrey's umbrella company, MagicLab, where he served as CEO.

In 2019 Andrey was publicly accused of creating a hostile work environment against women in the company. A UK law firm investigated the matter and cleared him of most accusations but suggested changes in the work environment.[10] Within days, the Blackstone Group bought out Andrey and named Whitney CEO of MagicLab, which she renamed to Bumble Inc. before taking it public the following year.

Whitney cofounded not one but two of the most popular online dating communities in the world, and she did it by adapting, changing, and focusing on building *her* way. Rather than allow what existed before to stand, she found ways to bend the trajectory through sheer will and ingenuity. From visiting college campuses and making Tinder go viral among an influential demographic to changing online dating by allowing women to make the first move, she built world-changing products without a technical background or experience. Throughout it all, she believed in her ability to solve real problems in the dating world. She trusted her instincts to guide her to where she is today.

Learning to Overcome Obstacles

In your life story, there will be an arc, one you can't see until well after the time has passed. Riding on the New York Metro, you can get from Rockefeller Center in Manhattan to Queens on the F train. But what you don't realize as you are on the train is that it turns a full ninety degrees to the right to get you there. The subway car moves, but you can't tell when the turn has taken you across the East River because you see only your progress relative to your position on the train. As you live your life, you will take major turns as circumstances change in your personal and professional life. Your ability to adapt and grow through those changes will determine your ultimate destination.

Lenore Blum was a pioneer in the field of mathematics and computer science and an accidental activist. She came of age at a time when women faced loss over and over due to the structures of society. Born in New York in 1942 during World War II, Lenore showed her aptitude for math early. By sixteen, she had enrolled in Carnegie Mellon University in Pittsburgh for architecture, but she did not take to it. Married at eighteen, Lenore transferred to Simmons College, where she met Dr. Marion Walter. Dr. Walter suggested Lenore attend MIT and secured her a place under the renowned mathematician Dr. Isadore Singer. Dr. Singer's class inspired her to apply to the MIT math PhD program. But when she went to meet with a professor in the MIT math department, he gave her a list and said, "If I had a daughter who was going to graduate school, these are the places I'd tell her to go. *MIT is not a place for women.*"

A week later, at a faculty party, that professor shared an amusing anecdote about a woman who had the audacity to apply to the PhD program. Dr. Singer asked who the professor was talking about. When he heard her name, Singer replied, "She's the best student in my class." Lenore was extended a place the next day.

With a PhD from MIT and a postdoc position under her belt, Lenore could go anywhere. She and her husband decided on Berkeley, but what she encountered there shocked her. She arrived to learn that no woman had been hired in the Berkeley math department for over two decades.

Growing up as a math wunderkind fostered by mentors and teachers, Lenore ran into obstacle after obstacle. She couldn't understand why she struggled when she had the same qualifications as her male peers. Offered an assistant professorship at Yale, Lenore turned it down to stay at Berkeley because her husband was a tenured professor in electrical engineering and computer science there, and they had a two-year-old son. Lenore taught for two more years at Berkeley, but when her third year came up, they passed on renewing her.

Looking for another role, Lenore found a home at the nearby women's college, Mills, where she created their math / computer science department. The Mills College dean, unhappy Lenore was turning the college into a technology center, fired her. She sought help from her mentors, and soon she had the college president and several board members who were faculty at Stanford step in on her behalf. Not only did Mills rescind her firing, but they also created an endowed professorship to keep her on.

During this time, Lenore realized that girls were not studying enough math in high school to enter STEM fields in college. So with Nancy Kreinberg and Rita (Liff) Levinson of the Lawrence

Hall of Science, Lenore helped create the Expanding Your Horizons Network (EYHN) in 1974. This new organization received a grant from the Carnegie Corporation of New York. Expanding Your Horizons created a network of women across the country to host conferences for middle and high school girls to encourage them to take science and math classes. Over the group's forty-year history, more than a million girls, especially those from less privileged backgrounds, have participated in their conferences and learned about STEM as a career choice. Many women who enter the field talk about having discovered STEM because of the work of Expanding Your Horizons.

I met Lenore Blum at the fortieth-anniversary celebration of the founding of Expanding Your Horizons Network, where I served for several years on the nonprofit board of directors. She and the other founders shared why they created EYHN and discussed their passion to bring more women into fields where they were pioneers. Lenore said, "When we started this organization forty years ago, we never thought it would take this long to solve these problems. Many of us are nearing retirement, and these issues still persist. We still have so much work to do after all this time."

Her words have stuck with me. These were women who faced discrimination to get into top STEM programs and then had to fight for jobs in a male-dominated environment. But they had hope for the next generation, and they worked toward equality for their whole careers.

Rather than getting stuck, they created networks to change the system. Lenore did not start out as an activist, but she became one when she saw the inequality around her. She found like-minded women and cofounded organizations, including the Association for Women in Mathematics and Expanding Your Horizons Network.

When she and her husband returned to Carnegie Mellon's computer science department, where her son was a tenured professor, she created Women@SCS to help equalize the number of women and men in the School of Computer Science. Whereas most CS departments enrolled less than 20 percent women, her work led to Carnegie Mellon being one of the first and few schools with gender parity. These networks went on to help women find their places in STEM, long after Lenore moved on.

Each time Lenore ran into an obstacle, she overcame those challenges by learning new ways to solve her problems. She sought allies and created networks, then put them to work helping others. Her grit and tenacity touched the lives of more than a million girls through EYHN, and her work at Carnegie Mellon showed that the computer science field can and will achieve gender equality. Today, even retired and in her seventies, Lenore is still learning and pioneering. She and her husband are now forging a new field to create a conscious Turing machine, which seeks to use math to model consciousness in artificial intelligence.

Breaking Through

A 2021 study from the executive recruiting firm Spencer Stuart showed that first-time CEOs outperform those who are leading their second company.[11] I read this report when I was deciding whether to take the offer to become the CEO of Ancestry. The finding felt counterintuitive to everything I was hearing from the executive recruiters I was working with as I explored these roles. Search firms repeatedly told me of great opportunities but warned that most boards would likely want someone who had held the top position before. I didn't fit the bill.

The study pointed out something akin to what the marshmallow-and-spaghetti-tower test did. It showed that those with a beginner's mind are more adaptable and more willing to pursue ideas beyond cost-cutting and efficiency gains. They are explorers, like the kindergarteners, rather than experts, like the MBAs, but boards still prefer those who are seasoned. That thought stuck in the back of my mind.

When I was approached to interview for a public company CEO position in 2020, we were days away from the pandemic lockdown. I didn't feel qualified to throw my hat in the ring, so I hesitated. Jim Citrin, the well-known Silicon Valley recruiter for boards and CEOs, asked if we could go to dinner to discuss it. As we were discussing the opportunity, I asked him, "Why me?"

His response was, "Why not you?"

I didn't know how to reply. Here was a respected Silicon Valley leader telling me that something I hadn't thought was possible was actually within reach. Jim went on to say, "Every single CEO had to get their first CEO job at some point. This is your chance."

I paused, thought about his words, and decided to apply. Through that grueling process, I learned so much about what a board is looking for, how to frame my ideas, and how to convince a group of people that I, someone who looks very little like a typical American CEO, could lead a company.

Though that role didn't work out, Jim's encouragement showed me that I had allowed myself to get stuck in the mindset that I wasn't good enough, that I didn't have the qualifications. By the time the CEO role for Ancestry came along, I had learned the skills necessary to land the job.

There will always be people who have more experience, who are smarter, or who are more qualified. No one sits at the pinnacle long because the world is changing too fast. The best skill you can have is the ability to learn how to learn.

Christine learned to be a CEO under the glare of #MeToo. Whitney lost everything, only to regain it by building her career and company her way. Lenore faced obstacle after obstacle, which led her to build an organization that has touched the lives of over a million girls. Each responded to their circumstances, leveraging them not as barriers but as challenges. Those challenges ended up defining their careers.

In small and big ways, you will face hardship. You will stumble. You will fail. But what you learn in those moments will ultimately determine what path you take going forward. You won't know it at the time because you won't sense the train turning to leave Manhattan and crossing the East River, but when you emerge on the other side, you will be in a different place. What that place looks like is up to you.

Learn to Forgive

*You don't choose what happens to you, but you have
the power to choose how you are affected by it.*
—NONA JONES

On June 17, 2015, Polly Sheppard attended Bible study at Emanuel African Methodist Episcopal (AME) Church. That night, Dylann Roof, a self-professed white supremacist, arrived and spent an hour in the study with his victims before pulling out a gun during prayer time. In all, he shot twelve people, nine of whom lost their lives, including Emanuel AME pastor and State Senator Clementa C. Pinckney. Polly witnessed her friends being gunned down in front of her, and when Dylann reached her, she recalled him saying, "I'm not going to shoot you. I'm going to leave you here to tell the story."[1]

Dylann Roof wanted to start a race war that day. He chose Emanuel AME—also known as Mother Emanuel, the oldest AME church in the South—as the spark to ignite that war. But what he encountered was something wholly different. Though he meant to terrorize and devastate, relatives and friends of the victims stood up one by one just a few days later in court and told him they forgave him. They released the poison that he had inflicted on their community, taking that anger and turning it into grace. News of their act of forgiveness took over the news and drowned out Roof's message of hate.[2]

I met Polly at a private screening of *Emanuel*, a movie about the shooting. I sat next to her, and as we watched the movie side by side, I sensed her peace, even as the terrible events of that day unfolded on screen. To be willing to relive the worst day of your life over and over and still speak up about how love could triumph over hate took an act of courage I could barely conceive.

June 17, 2015, was also the day that allowed Polly to find her voice. It wasn't an easy process. The anger and depression were all-consuming. At first she wasn't sure if she was ready to forgive Roof's actions, but she ultimately found an inner strength in the act of forgiveness. This led her to share her story over the next five years. A year after the shooting, at the Democratic National Convention, she said, "To heal, we must forgive. That is what I learned this past year. The shooter in Charleston had hate in his heart. The shooter in Orlando had hate in his heart. And the shooter in Dallas did, too. So much hate, too much. But as Scripture says, love never fails. So I choose love."[3]

Polly took back her power through forgiveness. She couldn't undo what had been done, but she could rise above it and bring some good out of it. "By taking back my power," she said, "I realize that I am not a victim. I am victorious. I had faith before, but now I have gained much more faith and strength."

Knowing she couldn't change the past, Polly decided to change the future instead. By turning her worst moments into something she would spend the rest of her life sharing with the world, she brought light out of the darkness. Her words and testimony helped heal a nation struggling with gun violence and racial tension. Now in her mid-seventies, she continues that journey by helping raise money to fund young people who want to enter nursing, specifically serving in the prison system, where she spent her career.

Forgiveness Is Freedom

Most of us will never face the stark reality of watching our friends die, of having to decide how to forgive what feels unforgivable. But for many of us, in each of our hearts, there is someone or something that holds us back, and those wounds continue to fester.

As the most senior member of the Christians at Facebook community, I was invited to be the opening speaker at the *Emanuel* movie screening, nearly four years to the day after the shooting. At first I considered turning it down. What the organizers didn't know was that I had grown up in a town outside Charleston, less than twenty miles from where the shooting happened, and I had avoided going back for two decades.

The amount of verbal abuse and threats I received during my childhood scarred me in ways I never allowed myself to process. I had never fully come to terms with what it was like to grow up experiencing that level of mistreatment, and so I coped with it through avoidance. But it still haunted me. To stand on a stage and speak about the ultimate forgiveness of families who had lost those they loved felt contradictory when I myself had never come to terms with the trauma of my childhood. This discrepancy forced me to take a long, hard look at how much anger I still harbored. Sitting next to Polly, hugging her during the movie, and watching her tell her story to the world taught me what true grace looks like. If she could look back with dignity and forgiveness, then I could do no less.

Forgiveness creates its own power and soothes the pain of old wounds. It allows us to break free of the hold the past has over us. But it isn't easy. I wish I could say that that one moment of decision changed everything, but I had yet to learn that forgiveness is both a choice and a process. Like any other kind of healing, it happens over time. The catharsis is gradual; it teaches us patience as we learn to let go of our pain.

Imagine the hurt of being wronged as a snake's fang embedded in your skin. As long as it's there, the poison continues to infect you, and the wound can't heal. Your suffering continues, and resentment grows. The pain of removing the fang—of choosing to forgive—can be immense in the moment, but its benefits to your psyche cannot be overstated. It not only gives you a chance to heal and recover, but it stops the poison from continuing to enter your body. No longer festering, the wound can now close as your body filters out the remaining resentment, anger, and distress. Removing the fang is the first step to becoming whole again.

Though forgiveness is a powerful force, in American society it is sometimes viewed as a weakness, as if by forgiving someone, we are letting them off the hook for their transgressions. What we don't realize is that forgiveness is for the forgiver, not for the forgiven. Not only does it yield psychological benefits, but it also yields physical and emotional dividends.

Dr. Loren Toussaint, professor of psychology at Luther College, has studied forgiveness for over two decades. According to his research, those who score high on measures of forgiveness showed evidence of major personal benefits, especially to mental health. In one study, his team demonstrated that among those living with a high level of stress, those who also exhibited high levels of forgiveness had fewer negative mental health outcomes.[4] Simply put, forgiveness protects our minds from the negative consequences of stress. Further studies Toussaint performed show that forgiveness in the workplace is associated with a 25 percent increase in productivity. This means that a workplace where people are more forgiving of one another is one that also produces better results—for both the forgiver and their company.[5]

Not everyone is asked to offer the grand gesture of forgiveness that Polly has displayed, but a grand gesture isn't always necessary. Freedom is pulling out the snake's fang to stop the resentment and pain from stealing your peace of mind. Only in this way can we process the hurt and find a path to peace.

Forgiving Yourself Is Part of the Process

Rowena Chiu spent two decades in the workforce and built an impressive résumé. Her accomplishments read as something most young women could only dream of: She graduated from the University of Oxford, going on to earn master's degrees from both the University of London and the London Business School. She lived in cities all over the world and worked at storied institutions, including McKinsey & Company, PricewaterhouseCoopers, and the World Bank. Today she lives with her equally successful husband and four children in the heart of Silicon Valley.

Despite her obvious achievements, Rowena kept a secret from everyone around her. When she first graduated from college, she accepted a dream position as the assistant to media mogul and Miramax Films cofounder Harvey Weinstein. It was the break she had dreamed of, a chance to get a foot in the door of the entertainment industry. After months of working with Rowena, teasing and grooming her, Weinstein finally cornered her at the Venice Film

Festival, attempting to rape her in a hotel room. Rowena managed to get away, but no one she reported the assault to, whether Miramax executives or the authorities, took action. She faced a team of Weinstein's lawyers, who bullied her into a settlement and a nondisclosure agreement. And thus began her silence.

As Rowena wrote in the *New York Times* article where she shared her story, "I spent decades grappling with guilt that I took the job, that I hadn't left the room sooner, that it was somehow my fault, that I hadn't handled Harvey 'robustly' enough, that I was not tough enough to work in the film industry."[6]

Harvey Weinstein and those around him took away more than Rowena's power. They took away her voice, her truth. The nondisclosure agreement not only stopped her from speaking publicly; it also meant she couldn't tell a therapist, doctor, pastor, or even her spouse without fear of repercussions. For twenty years she stayed silent, afraid to break the contract. Unable to find work, she ended up in Miramax's realm again, this time in Hong Kong. The silence and isolation took their toll. Two suicide attempts later, Rowena left everything behind and started over in London in a corporate environment where she felt she would be safer.

When reporters Jodi Kantor, Megan Twohey, and Ronan Farrow initially reached out, Rowena refused to go public with her story. Then, in early 2019, things changed. She joined a group of women, all part of the #MeToo movement, at Gwyneth Paltrow's house. There she met Dr. Christine Blasey Ford, who testified in the confirmation hearing of then–Supreme Court nominee Brett Kavanaugh. Dr. Ford's story inspired Rowena to overcome her fear and speak out. A couple of months later, Rowena was invited to speak before the Women and Equalities Committee in the House of Commons in the United Kingdom. There she learned that by telling her story, she could take back her power from Harvey Weinstein and his enablers. This led her to change her mind and agree to be included in Kantor and Twohey's book about Harvey Weinstein, *She Said*. Rowena knew this meant she would have to tell her friends and family before the book came out in September. On October 5, 2019, Rowena took control of the narrative and wrote an editorial in the pages of the *New York Times*, recounting her experience. On that day, she went from silence to sharing her story with the whole world.

The impact was immediate. Dozens of women, especially Asian American women like her, reached out to share their stories of assault and the subsequent shame that accompanied them. Her published words enabled her to take control of her own story and help others overcome the guilt of being victims of sexual assault.

When asked how women who face similar circumstances can take back their power, Rowena said, "Silence never benefits anyone except your perpetrator. And the silence can destroy you. Your story matters. Your voice matters. Your life matters. And speaking out could change everything: for you, for others, for our society. The #MeToo movement is about women becoming empowered, women speaking out, and women taking back their power. It means that our stories—our meaning, our lives—are no longer in the shadows."

Rowena's journey was not only about forgiving Harvey Weinstein and his enablers but also learning to forgive herself. For years she wondered if there was more she could have done. The contract she had signed locked her in a place of shame and stress. Thoughts of "what if?" ran through her head for the duration of her long silence. If only she could have gotten someone to listen, she thought. If only she had negotiated her settlement harder to get accountability. If only she could have stopped him twenty years ago. But in the end, Rowena realized she was living within the wrong framing of her experiences. By assuming responsibility for what subsequently happened, she unwittingly took on guilt for something beyond her control, causing herself more pain.

Forgiving yourself is often the hardest type of forgiveness. Many people, especially women, ruminate on what has gone wrong. We wish we could rewrite history, do it better. But instead of saying, "I am unforgiving to myself," we talk about the pain of the past in the form of a single, seemingly innocuous word: *regret*. Regret is a slow-acting poison that is framed by the recurrent thought of *if only*. At first, thinking over a decision or event feels harmless, but over time, that rumination infects our lives.

When we feel regret, we are wishing for another outcome, another timeline to unfold from the moment when a tragedy happened. It's a fantasy of second chances. In the 1998 movie *Sliding Doors*, a young woman, played by Gwyneth Paltrow, misses her train, and one version of the story is told from there on. But then the movie rewinds, changing the outcome so that she makes the train. A second story then unfolds on a split screen between the different timelines, showing two parallel versions of her reality. In the end, she arrives in the same place, but one of the two timelines ends tragically and is terminated. This is an illustration of the allure of *if only*: it allows us to imagine new versions of reality, to fantasize about what our lives would be like if past events had gone differently.

Sanyin, the overachiever from chapter 3 who was forced to create her own path, felt this regret acutely. Losing her scholarship to Duke University in her junior year and not making it to medical school haunted her for years. Even with everything she achieved in the next two decades, she felt like an impostor. She saw herself as the girl who had failed. But as the years passed, she realized that her regret was largely unproductive and self-defeating. She came to terms with it this way: "I think if we love the good in our lives now, we can't regret what came before it. The joys and griefs are all a part of what brings us to the here and now. And there is a lot of good that I love now that I would not trade for changing the past." She realized that her *Sliding Doors* moment wouldn't have brought her to the successful place she is today, where she coaches CEOs, famous athletes, and military generals.

By allowing regret to seep in, we torture ourselves with the idea of changing the past. In doing so, we forget that looking backward means we can't look forward. Regret pushes us to want the do-over, the chance to relive the pivotal moments because we have yet to come to terms with the reality of our situation. We blame ourselves for the way things have turned out. This is exactly why self-forgiveness is so important. Rather than looking back at those moments as ones we wish we could change, we can instead view our negative experiences as steps that have led us to where we are today.

Maybe you regret staying too long in a bad relationship or missing out on a job or promotion. Maybe you regret the way you handled a certain situation or a choice you made that has impacted your life. At each major divergence in your path, there is always a road not taken, and it's easy to become lost thinking about the crossroads. But that doesn't bring you any closer to your destination. Moving on and forgiving yourself means being able to walk forward with clarity, rather than spending your life looking back over your shoulder.

While I have largely been able to process my biggest regrets with the benefit of hindsight, a lot of the small ones have plagued me. I've left meetings kicking myself for not sharing my idea more forcefully, for letting someone—usually a man—interrupt me. I've regretted the ways I've pitched my ideas. Some nights I've lain awake in bed, staring at the ceiling, running these mistakes through my mind over and over.

One day I realized that these obsessive thoughts were anchoring me in place, and I couldn't pull free.

The moment that changed my mindset was when my son, Jonathan, was born. I knew that moms were often plagued with guilt and regret, and so I actively decided to raise him and any other future children without that negative energy in our lives. From the moment he came into the world, I willed myself to look forward and not back. If I made a mistake and scolded him too strongly, I sat him down and apologized and worked on being better. If I spent too little time with him because I had to travel, I invested more time the next week. Rather than ruminating over my past mistakes, I decided to instead focus my energy on setting things right. This was freeing as a mom, and so I decided to adopt this same outlook in my life and work.

Forgiveness as a Tool to Take Back Your Power

Nona Jones is a renowned pastor, influencer, and founder of Faith & Prejudice, an organization that encourages conversations focused on the church and racial justice. She is also the head of Faith Partnerships at Facebook. Her journey forced her to learn forgiveness.

Nona's mother didn't want children, but her father was excited about having a daughter. Tragically, however, he was diagnosed with cancer partway through her mother's pregnancy, and Nona lost him when she was two. Her mother dealt with the loss by moving to a whole new place and started dating a new man when Nona was five. That was when the sexual abuse began. Nona was a vulnerable child who had lost her father, only to face a predator in her own home. He was taken to jail several years later, after she worked up the courage to tell her mom about the abuse, and Nona thought she was free. Soon after, however, her mother brought the man back into their home, and the abuse started up again.

Deep in despair about the abuse and her mother's betrayal, Nona attempted suicide twice before she turned eleven. It was then that she found faith through the church, which helped her cope with the abuse until she left home for college.

Nona never planned to tell her story. When a college roommate opened up to her about her rape, Nona tried to comfort her, only to experience pushback that she could not possibly understand what it was like to be raped. This was what prompted Nona to share her own story of childhood sexual abuse, and she saw firsthand how the power of sharing her experience was transformative and healing for her roommate. From then on, Nona continued to open up about her story. By leaning into her trauma, she learned to use it as a positive force in her life.

Nona now shares her experience widely to help those who have faced similar abuse. She has developed a podcast, written three books, and is a major influencer in ministry. All of this was possible because she took the worst thing that ever happened to her and turned it into an impetus to power her forward. She has extended forgiveness to her mother and her boyfriend for their abuse and neglect, and that has freed her from the weight of anger and despair. Her forgiveness was not about them; it was always about her own ability to move forward in the world.

We can choose to be the victim or beneficiary of our history and experiences. During those dark childhood years, Nona was the victim, but then she took control of her story and used it as a catalyst to become who she is today. She took back her power by leveraging her past to become the author of her own story.

What Forgiveness Is Not

Forgiveness is often misunderstood, and knowing and understanding what it *isn't* is just as important as knowing and understanding what it is.

Forgiveness is not instantaneous. Rather, it is a process. We tend to imagine forgiveness as a single moment, a cathartic event when everything is fixed with some magic wand that takes away the hurt. Instead, it requires investment and effort. It can take months, even years. As Polly recounts, "Forgiveness is a process. You can forgive one day and be angry the next day. It gets better with time. You have to get rid of the hatred and malice in your heart. If you don't get rid of the hatred, that person has power over you."

Forgiveness is first and foremost for the benefit of the forgiver, not the forgiven. Many times, the person who hurt you will never apologize for, or even acknowledge, their role in your pain. Harvey Weinstein never acknowledged the hurt and damage he did. In fact, he is appealing his conviction, even after more than eighty women have come forward to accuse him of misconduct.[7] Forgiveness is not excusing bad behavior. Rather, it is changing your mindset toward the offender so you can move on with your life without anger and bitterness.

Forgiveness is not justice, nor does it eschew justice. Just because someone forgives those who hurt them does not mean no justice is required. These two concepts aren't mutually exclusive. Forgiveness means that there is no malice in the heart toward the offender, but still allows for the offender to be held accountable. The families of those at Emanuel offered grace but also sought justice in the courts for their loved ones. After the testimony of those who bore witness, the jury found Dylann Roof guilty of thirty-three charges against him in a mere two hours. A judge then sentenced him to death by lethal injection.[8]

Forgiveness is not reconciliation, nor does it require a relationship with the offender. While forgiveness opens the door to restoration, it doesn't necessarily mean the relationship is healed. As Nona explained, "While forgiveness is our power, reconciliation is not based on forgiveness alone. Reconciliation requires both forgiveness and repentance. My mother has never repented for what she did and allowed, which is why we are not in a relationship today." Nona chose to forgive, but she severed ties with her mother and her boyfriend because they never acknowledged how he hurt her. This allowed her to release her resentment toward them and move forward without their toxic influence in her life.

Forgiveness at Work

Conflict at work is inevitable, but left unaddressed, it can lead to withdrawal, poor productivity, and increased stress. Even so, forgiveness in the workplace is doubly hard. Unlike in our personal relationships, where we can minimize contact or cut someone who hurt us out of our lives, at work we are often forced to engage repeatedly with those who have offended us. The frustration and hurt remain each time we see them. The poison continues to seep in. Resentment grows, and this emotional baggage builds up over time.

I once had a major interpersonal conflict at work, and every subsequent time I encountered that colleague, I added more grievances to my list. One day, when I vented to my career coach about how upset I was, she calmly asked, "When are you going to put down the backpack?"

I looked at her, confused. She explained: "Each time you pick up another grievance, it is a stone you pick up and put in your backpack. As you walk, the backpack gets heavier and heavier, but you are the one carrying it, not them."

Taking back your power is not about excusing others' behavior; instead, it is about ridding yourself of the backpack you carry. Toussaint and his colleagues conducted research at Ameriprise Financial, where over a six-to-nine-month period, groups were taught about forgiveness in the workplace and then provided follow-up calls and support. Those who completed the program saw their productivity increase by 24 percent, versus only 10 percent for those not participating. Program participants also saw their stress levels decrease and their quality of life improve.[9] These workers put down their metaphorical backpacks, and that led to better outcomes for both them and the company.

According to Toussaint's research, women benefit from forgiveness even more than men. As he shared with me, "Women who were higher in forgiveness of others had a greater drop in risk of depression than men. Knowing how important one's mental health is to overall health and productivity, women should use this knowledge to motivate forgiveness. It truly does help you feel better, and feeling better often means you work better."

Forgiveness and Reconciliation

I once had a relationship with a colleague so challenging that it almost drove me to quit my job. What followed was a lesson in reconciliation, resilience, and making challenging relationships work.

Six years ago I was meeting up with my then-manager, Mike Vernal. He had just returned from parental leave, and he shared his thoughts on being a first-time father and being away from work for so long. He then told me he was leaving the company. I was floored. Mike had been my manager and sponsor for years, and he was one of the most stable management relationships I had at the company. I paused for a moment and held my breath. His next words hit me hard.

"You will report to Boz."

Andrew "Boz" Bosworth was the well-respected leader of the ads team, but we did not get along. While I was on a different team, platform, I had cocreated Facebook's first ads vertical: mobile app ads. Our teams had to partner closely, so our success depended on our cooperation. Boz's shoot-from-the-hip, aggressive work style rubbed me the wrong way. His big and extroverted personality meant that when we were in meetings together, he would speak over me, making it hard to make my voice heard. In response, I would shrink back. I found him intimidating, and he found me evasive. The more he pushed, the more I retreated. This went on for years. I trained myself to sit across from him so that I could gauge his reaction to every word I said and stay ahead of criticism. Unbeknownst to either of us, I was terrified of him because his personality reminded me of the boys who taunted me when I was growing up.

As a product manager, I had been doing my own form of A/B testing on our relationship, where I tried different actions to see if things would change. I tried proactive engagement, and it resulted in a series of frustrating conversations. I then tried avoiding him whenever possible, a strategy that ended up being punctuated by a series of disagreements that our teams witnessed. I eventually chalked up our relationship difficulties to our differing worldviews, styles, and life experiences, and I decided to give up any interaction unless strictly necessary.

Our relationship was so contentious that Sheryl Sandberg, the chief operating officer of Facebook, eventually pulled us aside and asked us to sit down for several mediation sessions with Fred Kofman, author of the book *Conscious Business*. We needed outside help to learn to work together without as much visible tension. While the mediations helped us coexist, we still kept a polite distance from each other. We had learned to work together but had not yet resolved the root cause of our disagreements.

I loved my job. I enjoyed the people and loved that we were building impactful products. It was just a few weeks before I was to go on stage at F8, Facebook's annual developer conference, which I helped organize. And yet, with the news that Boz was to be my new manager, I was one day away from quitting. I vividly remember calling my husband to tell him I needed to find a new job. David, knowing how I felt about Boz, was surprised but supportive.

But before I could finalize my decision, several other senior leaders, including the CEO, intervened and asked us to sit down and talk through our problems. When Sheryl asked me to give my relationship with Boz a chance, I told her he was the one person I would rather quit than work for and asked her what she would do if faced with the same situation. She replied that she believed Boz and I had a lot to teach each other. Out of respect for Sheryl and for the sake of my team, I agreed to give the relationship another shot. Boz and I sat down together and discussed the possibility of continuing to work together.

It turned out that he had been as surprised as I was by the news that my team was going to be moved to his in the aftermath of Mike's departure. And he had as much trepidation about working together as I did. What followed this realization was one of the hardest conversations I've ever had. We rehashed years of contention and disagreement. I shared with him through tears how I was scared of him, and he was shocked and apologetic. My relationship with my manager has always been extremely important to me, and I told him that I would rather quit than work for him. Despite all this, Boz felt we could still make it work somehow.

I was bullied through much of my childhood, and I felt like working with someone who pushed my buttons, even unintentionally, would make me miserable. We respected each other from a distance, but we had never figured out how to work together despite honest effort on both sides. We were so different that every conversation was fraught with pitfalls, and after four years of this, we struggled to find common ground. Our backpacks were full of resentment and misunderstandings.

The biggest revelation about our relationship was that I had harbored a great deal of resentment against Boz over many years. I had been placing the blame entirely on his actions, without factoring in my own reactions to what he did and how he acted. When we spoke, really spoke, that was the first time I acknowledged this to myself or anyone else. I shared how I felt, and he accepted it with regret since he had no idea that I had interpreted his actions in such a negative way. In turn, the steps I took to distance myself from him made me seem very challenging to partner with from his perspective. It was only through this discussion that we were able to identify what had caused the barriers in our relationship.

After getting to the root of the problem, Boz and I came up with a plan to repair our relationship and turn over a new leaf. We committed to each other to do two things:

- immediately and honestly speak up if we felt something was off
- go out of our way to give each other the benefit of the doubt

What started as a single conversation about forgiveness turned into a process of reconciliation. Building a productive partnership didn't happen overnight, and several times over the next few months, we had to rely on our commitment to resolve new conflicts that arose. Each time we refused to allow the past to taint the present, that allowed us to build a foundation to move forward. This relationship worked only because it was what we both sought earnestly. Not only did Boz and I find mutual forgiveness, but several of my most productive years at Facebook were under his leadership.

A few years later, and during our regular one-on-one, Boz told me he was leaving the team to go run the new Facebook Reality Labs, home to our augmented and virtual reality products. To my surprise, and I suspected also his, my reaction was one of genuine sadness. I blurted out, "I know you are going to be surprised to hear me say this, but I'm sad we will not be working together closely anymore." I meant it. Boz smiled and told me he wasn't surprised at all because he felt the same way.

When I asked him if I could include this story in a book, he graciously said yes. During my time reporting to him, he encouraged me to write and share my experiences, something he had done over many years. Over the next several years since I started reporting to him, I wrote dozens of articles, which ultimately led me to write this book. When I told him that, he replied, "This is the best ending to our story."

Steps toward Forgiveness

Acknowledge the Hurt

Without a full understanding of the scope of your pain, you can't see the damage it has caused. Without understanding the damage, you can't heal. Sometimes looking directly at the pain can feel terrifying, but avoiding it means not facing the truth of what happened. On a piece of paper, start by writing down the story of the hurt you've experienced, and allow the words to be part of your journey. By doing so, you force yourself to acknowledge the hurt and face the pain head-on.

Decide to Move On

Give yourself the time and space to mourn the event or relationship. Then take the paper where you wrote down your story and burn it or tear it up. This ritual gives you a physical act to remember when you decide to forgive. Each time the memories and pain return, remember the moment you destroyed the hurt and released yourself. It will be a process, and it is not instantaneous, but deciding to move on is an important step to reframing the way you address your experience.

Step Forward toward Your Goals

You will always stumble if you are looking backward while walking forward. Look ahead and move toward the future you want. Without the weight of the past holding you back, you are free to embark on the next part of your journey. The past is behind you, and there are new possibilities ahead.

As counterintuitive as it may seem, forgiving yourself and those who hurt you is an important step to taking back your power. Harboring regret and resentment over past events is a slow-acting poison, one that negatively impacts your quality of life in the long term, despite seeming to be an easier path. Think of forgiveness as a gift you give yourself: it is permission to put down the backpack, to heal, and to move forward with your life, unburdened by *what ifs* and *if onlys*.

There is great potential for personal growth in being able to remove the shackles of the past. But it starts only when you forgive yourself and those who hurt you. The act of letting go enables you to take back your power, to live your life free of resentment. The power is in your hands.

Develop Allies

Though one may be overpowered,
two can defend themselves.
A cord of three strands is not quickly broken.
—Ecclesiastes 4:12

Several months after I joined the executive team at Facebook, my manager, Mike Vernal, asked me why I never spoke up at our weekly meetings. I was surprised he didn't know, so I asked him to observe the next meeting.

Afterward, he said, "I never noticed this before, but you were interrupted every time you spoke."

I replied, "See why I don't speak up more?" All this time, I assumed he knew but didn't care. A few weeks later, in a discussion with this same group, I was asked about my product. Suddenly, a male colleague jumped in and not only interrupted me but also explained my product to the forum. Embarrassed and unsure of what to do, I ceded the floor to him. It was a classic moment of giving away my power to a more imposing man in the room.

That night, I got a message from that colleague apologizing for interrupting me. I was caught off guard since this was not the first time we'd had this type of interaction. I later found out that Mike had reached out to him and pointed out what he observed, and from then on this colleague stopped interrupting me.

This is what an ally looks like.

No one succeeds alone. Allies are some of the most important partners in a successful career journey, particularly for women. Throughout your career, you will meet a handful of people who accelerate your career, give you opportunities, and push you to be more than you ever imagined. These people are your peers, your managers, and your sponsors. They are the ones who believe in you more than you believe in yourself. They are there to help you through challenges and celebrate your achievements. They are your cheer section, your coaches, and your partners.

The path to success is not linear, and often the journey will take you down winding roads. Knowing someone has your back allows you to explore paths that aren't as clear-cut. Having allies gives you the courage to take risks and explore because you know that if you stumble or fall, someone will be there to catch you.

There are four main groups of allies in the workforce. Creating and nurturing these relationships will transform your career.

- mentors
- sponsors
- teams
- circles

---

mentor

|'men.tôr,'men(t)ər|

noun

an experienced and trusted adviser[1]

The word *mentor* comes from the name of a character in Homer's *Odyssey*. A friend of Odysseus, Mentor was tasked with helping to guide Odysseus's son, Telemachus, while his father, the king of Ithaca, was away fighting the Trojan War. However, Mentor turned out to be a poor guide. Athena, the Greek goddess of wisdom, took his form and intervened to imbue Telemachus with mental strength and life direction.[2] Mentor was thus popularized as the name of someone who is a guide for another.

Mentors can play an important role in your career and be instrumental in helping you take back your power. They are advisors and guides in the workplace, and they provide insight and help as you navigate your choices. Yet 63 percent of women report never having had a formal mentor in their careers.[3] These women are missing out on an important ally and a critical relationship. Mentors are teachers, coaches, and advisors all at once. A great mentor holds you accountable and expands your horizons.

A long-term study from the mid-2000s done at Sun Microsystems found that those with a mentor stayed at the company at a 23 percent higher rate (72 percent versus 49 percent for those without a mentor). One in four of those mentored was promoted at least once during the study period, which was five times the rate of those not a part of the program.[4] That means that having a mentor improved outcomes for participants by 400 percent!

A Cornell study found that formal mentoring programs improve overall retention, help people reach management, and accelerate promotions. Interestingly, these effects are most pronounced with women. Researchers believe mentors offer individuals from diverse backgrounds access to advancement opportunities. Without these programs, many women and minorities would not have advanced nearly as quickly.[5] Despite the obvious benefits, only about half of organizations have formal mentoring programs, and often women need to take back their power by creating and finding mentors on their own.

Throughout my eighteen-year career in tech, I have mentored and been mentored by many people. Each relationship has brought new ideas and experiences into my life and taught me lessons that I've taken with me.

Get Help Finding the Right Match

While many mentoring relationships grow organically, you can speed up the process by asking someone you trust to help you find a mentor. They can help match you with the right person and set up the relationship for success.

When I find mentors for people on my team, for example, the first thing I do is learn what they hope to get out of the relationship. Once I understand that, I suggest mentors who match their interests and goals. I then go a step further and make the ask on their behalf. Many of these senior leaders will make time to mentor someone I recommend because they know I have vetted the mentee for a learning mindset and desire to grow. They also know that the mentee is accountable to me for their continued engagement in the mentoring process.

I asked Brady Lauback, a senior data science leader, to mentor the head of data science on my team, Ashish Nayyar. I saw a lot of potential in Ashish, but I needed someone from that field to help coach him and identify the work that needed to be done for him to be promoted.

A couple of years later, he reached out and remarked, "At first I was reluctant, but it was one of the most fulfilling things I had done lately." I had twisted his arm to do it, but I also knew he would be the perfect person to help Ashish grow in his career. I asked Brady about the experience, and he said, "This experience encouraged me to more naturally mentor other folks who were less like me, something I have sought out since."

Going through a "matchmaker" can also help you access mentors you might otherwise be unable to reach. In my own case, because of time constraints and how much I invest in these relationships, I can mentor only three to five people at a time. I used to be part of a program that assigned me a random mentee at the company, but I found those relationships to be somewhat unsatisfying for both of us; what I had to offer and what they needed were misaligned. I now take mentees only at the request of someone who knows both of us and knows that I can be of unique support to the mentee.

Nurture the Relationship

As in any relationship, building trust with your mentor is critical. Often when we're being mentored, we mistake it for a service someone is offering us. We ask for advice, and they give it to us. But mentoring is a relationship, not a transaction. If you treat mentorship as something you only receive, the relationship will quickly fizzle out.

Mentors usually sign up to help you through a problem, or if they go through a program, the relationship lasts for a set amount of time. They invest their own time and effort to support you. Your job is to make sure their investment is worthwhile and that you are giving back to them and also paying it forward to others.

As a mentor, I often wonder whether I'm having a positive impact, especially if I'm not getting any feedback. Having a mentee follow up and let me know they took the advice I gave them—and how it turned out—is gratifying. It makes me more invested in their success and our relationship.

Turn a Mentor into a Sponsor

Every mentor has different criteria—conscious or not—for deciding to invest in a mentee for the long haul. In general, however, they're looking for someone who not only shows promise but is actively working to live up to that promise. They want someone who is eager to take on stretch assignments and volunteer to contribute broadly, such as by running a new training or recruiting program. Each time you meet is a chance to demonstrate those traits to your mentor and proactively show them that you're worthy of sponsorship.

Mentorship is an important relationship from both sides. Yes, the mentor has to put a lot into it—but it's also up to the mentee to be thoughtful about what they put in and what they want to get out of it. By being a great mentee, you not only advance your career; you can learn the lessons you need to be a great mentor in the future too.

Not every workplace offers formal mentorship, but that doesn't mean you have to live without it. Seek out people in your network or industry you want to learn from, and ask them for advice. Even if it is a short-term relationship, their insights and support can help you through challenging times.

People don't have a clear distinction between what a mentor is and what a sponsor is. They are related but not the same. One thing I do during talks is ask who has had a sponsor. Usually, about 20 percent of the room raises their hands. The thing is, if you've had a sponsor, you know it. There is no mistaking it because while a mentor supports you and gives you advice, a sponsor lifts you up and opens doors.

---

sponsor

|'spänsər| |'spansər

noun

a person taking official responsibility for the actions of another[6]

Sponsors create opportunities. They invest their reputations to help you grow and advance. They point out hard truths and believe in your potential, often more than you believe in yourself.

Mentor	Sponsor
Gives advice	Opens doors
Makes suggestions	Shares hard feedback
Discusses your problems	Pushes you to strive for more
Says positive things when asked	Creates opportunities for you
Tells you to believe in yourself	Believes in your potential
Helps you out	Has your back
Suggests ways to get what you want	Advocates for you

Women Have Mentors, Men Have Sponsors

Men are 46 percent more likely to have a sponsor, according to Sylvia Ann Hewlett, author of *Forget a Mentor, Find a Sponsor*.[7] After studying sponsorship in nearly ten thousand employees in the US and the UK, Hewlett observed that sponsorship can increase the ability to land a raise or a stretch assignment by 30 percent. Women are more likely than men to have mentors, but they're not as likely to have sponsors. It is access to this transformative relationship that gives men a leg up in their careers.

Sponsorship is more than a one-sided relationship. Sponsors are more senior in the organization, often one or two levels up. They find people they connect with and look for ways to support them. They also get something important for their efforts: the ability to give back and receive recognition for identifying and growing new talent in the organization.

Sponsors put their reputations on the line for those they help, so it is natural they look for people most like them. Because men make up four out of five executives, men also make up a bulk of those with powerful sponsors. This can be a challenge for a woman seeking a sponsor. A study by LeanIn.Org and SurveyMonkey found that in 2019, 60 percent of male managers were hesitant to engage with women in work activities such as mentorship or working alone together.[8] This grew by 32 percent in just one year, as the #MeToo movement has scared senior men away from engaging with more junior women. These senior men are twelve times more hesitant to have one-on-one meetings with junior women versus junior men. But being a sponsor requires time together.

Sponsors Can Transform Your Career

Many people who have mentored me, like my early managers at Facebook, continued to advocate for me long after we met, eventually acting as sponsors for my career. They moved beyond the set engagement and turned into advocates. In turn, I sponsor many people I've mentored throughout my career, but not all of them. I look for people with initiative who are worth championing long after our initial relationship is complete. I started my product career at PayPal. There I met my first sponsor, Amy Klement, who was the vice president (VP) of product. She trusted me to help lead the integration between PayPal and eBay. When the time came to hire a new director to manage the PM team, she interviewed several senior-level candidates and then offered me the role. This was even though I had only three years of PM experience and had only just begun to manage people. Time and time again, when given a choice, she opened doors and accelerated my career, encouraging me to take on more responsibilities and giving me opportunities to learn new areas. When I asked her whether I should join Facebook after seven years at PayPal and eBay, she was the first to encourage me to take the risk.

Sponsors believe in you and in your ability to succeed, even when you don't believe in yourself. Doug Purdy, my seventh manager at Facebook, supported and encouraged me throughout the challenging period that followed Danielle's birth and my father's death. During our first conversation, he told me to trust him. Not once did he doubt that I could be successful, even though I doubted myself. He told me multiple times, "You will be a VP here someday," even though I had never been promoted in my two and a half years at the company, and I was not even a director. I laughed each time he said it and joked back that even he was not a VP at the time. But he believed in me and encouraged me even when I wasn't sure I could succeed. He advocated for me to take on more responsibilities, helped me get promoted, and eventually when he left the team, he made me his successor.

Shortly thereafter, Sheryl Sandberg introduced me to the CEO of Intuit, Brad Smith. She told me he came to Facebook to learn how we built products, and he wanted to learn about platforms and payments, two areas I led at the time. She pulled me aside and said, "If this goes well, maybe you can join their board someday." I laughed since it seemed far-fetched for a public company to be interested in me as a board member. Brad and I met and had a good conversation. Two years later, a board seat opened up, and again Sheryl put forth my name. She told me, "I can open the door, but you decide what you do with it."

I remember how nervous I was walking into Brad's office to meet with him. I had no idea what he was looking for, but I was pretty sure that I wasn't it. Wanting to do justice to Sheryl's faith in me, I decided to go for broke. I went into the meeting holding nothing back as I shared my insights on Intuit's strategy and products, products I had faithfully used and passionately evangelized for more than fifteen years. This was my one chance to share my point of view both as a long-time customer and a product leader. At the end of the conversation, Brad asked me if I wanted to join the board. I was shocked.

During that whole process, in the back of my mind, I knew I didn't want to disappoint Sheryl. She gave me an opportunity I could never have imagined, and my job was to justify her faith in me. Since joining the Intuit board, I have been invited to interview for many more boards, but I have limited capacity and time. I pay it forward with a board referral list of over a dozen board-ready candidates, many who were just like I was when Sheryl recommended me: full of raw potential and waiting for the right opportunity.

I have benefited greatly from having incredible sponsors. In turn, I sponsor people throughout the industry—especially women. When new opportunities arise, I put their names forward. I actively encourage them to take on roles they would have thought were beyond their reach. At times I help resolve conflicts or challenges that stand in their way. But I also give them hard feedback to ensure that they see their blind spots. I see my role as a mix of mentor, supporter, and motivator, but I always believe in their potential, often more than they do.

Sponsors Find You, Not the Other Way Around

Sponsorship is an incredibly important aspect of career growth and pursuing new opportunities, but it is not a relationship that is easily forged. Finding a sponsor can be challenging because it requires mutual trust and respect that is often built over a long period. Many sponsors start as managers, mentors, or cross-functional partners. They see your potential, value your contribution, and start helping you. Once created, this relationship dynamic extends even after you have moved on to new roles and opportunities.

Finding a sponsor is hard because it's not something you can simply ask for. Sponsors find you, not the other way around. Instead, start by building a relationship. Because the sponsor is advocating for you, your success is their success, and your failure is their failure. Your actions reflect directly on them, so trust is critical. They need to know that their investment in you is warranted and that you will live up to the potential they see in you. Look around for someone with whom you already have a strong relationship, and ask them for advice on how to grow. Then take that advice. Continue to seek out their advice, and continue to show them you are willing to be honest with yourself and address your blind spots. Prove to them that their time invested in you is worthwhile.

A Note on Queen Bee Syndrome

Popularized in the 1970s, queen bee syndrome is the idea that women are harder on other women. It comes from the notion that they are protecting their space in leadership by tamping down the careers of other women. Recent studies refute this. Queen bee syndrome does happen, but it presents itself when women are put into positions by male leaders who have an implicit quota.[9] Thus, another woman joining is set up as a threat. But when women are themselves in senior leadership, such as in the executive ranks or on the board, more women are promoted or reach positions of leadership.[10]

Women do pay a price for advocating for other women, yet in most circumstances, they still choose to do so. A study by researchers at the University of Colorado found that while men don't necessarily get credit for promoting diversity, women and minorities are actively punished for it in their performance reviews.[11] I remember once I was asked to take over a team where everyone had left and I needed to rebuild it from scratch. I hired three Asian American women onto my team in a row. The hiring procedures were fairly stringent, and the new hires were universally agreed upon as the best candidates for their respective jobs. My manager pulled me aside and warned me that I should be careful of the perception that this left, advising me to think carefully about my next hire. He was an ally and my sponsor, so in response, I asked, "Would you have said that if I hired three white men?"

He made a counterpoint by saying, "I understand, but others may not. I am only saying this because I have your best interests at heart." The sad part was he was right, yet wrong at the same time.

One final note on sponsors. When many people first hear about them, they wonder if the system is rigged so that some people can engage with sponsors while others can't. The reality is that the workplace is full of people who could be amazing sponsors for you, but sponsors tend to choose to support those most like them. Given the senior leadership demographics, this means that many potential sponsors are likely men, and thus male colleagues are much more likely to have access to them. These male allies, like Doug was for me, can play a critical role in your growth. Taking back your power means actively seeking out these relationships and finding ways to show that women are also worthy of this support, and then, when you achieve success, to pay it forward to the next generation.

---

team

|tēm|

noun

a number of persons associated together in work or activity[12]

Thriving through a Team

Who you work with is more important than what you work on. Finding a place where you can thrive is critical to your success, and that starts with your team. Often we pick a job because it is interesting or fits our skills, but when you choose a role or a company, think hard about the people you will work with. You will likely spend more waking time with them than your own spouse or family, and yet you may not always think about how the dynamics of your team will affect your life. Your teammates can be your best allies, but they can also be your worst enemies. Finding alignment is critical so that you are working together rather than competing.

Google looked at over 180 teams and tried to figure out what the most impactful and effective ones had in common.[13] Laszlo Bock published the results in the book *Work Rules!* If you imagine a great, well-functioning team, what do you picture? Is it a group of the smartest people? Is it a team of high performers? Perhaps it is diverse so that everyone brings a different point of view. Or maybe it's homogeneous so that everyone shares a similar background.

A great team is none of these things. Rather, it is not about *who* is on the team but *how* they choose to work together.

The key element cited for the most effective teams at Google was a simple one: psychological safety. Teams that create a culture of belonging enable members to take risks without fear of judgment. They can confront one another and have honest and hard conversations about what is going well and what isn't. If you are on a high-functioning team, you can feel it. Things are easy, and there is trust. They are your allies, lifting you up and helping you improve.

When you are operating in a poorly functioning team, everyone is there to protect themselves. There is friction and mistrust. I once had a team in my organization in which all our meetings felt fraught. They couldn't get on the same page, so they met one-on-one, creating factions and alliances to get support for their ideas. During meetings, they pretended to go along with the proposals and then undermined one another by instructing the teams they supported to do the opposite. My design director pointed out after one of the meetings, "It is downright chilly being in a room with them." Their interactions felt heavy, and everyone was stressed out. Needless to say, I had to reboot the group. Interestingly, the team members went on to other teams within the company where they didn't fall into these same negative patterns. Rather, they thrived in their new roles away from one another. This tells you that much of the issue was the culture they created with one another and not the people themselves.

When you find a team where there is trust, you will be among allies focused on the same goal. We have a rule in our organization called #saythething. Whenever there is a meeting or discussion, we all leave everything on the table. There are no sidebars, no outside-the-room lobbying. Everyone who has a say comes in and reviews the same materials, and we decide as a group. When we walk out, even if we don't agree with the decision, we allow ourselves to disagree and then commit.

Building Teams through Trust

Often women want to be liked and accepted, so we shy away from hard conversations where true alignment happens. But it is through these difficult situations and awkward conversations that trust is formed. One way a team is forged is to build something together. During my first few months as the CEO at Ancestry, I could sense that my leadership team still had not gelled. We tried working with an executive coach and spending time together, but it was not until we went through the fire of pulling together our first board presentation that we were able to put all our conflicts out in the open. When the team stared at the words of the final presentation together, we had to decide whether to link arms and commit to our new vision and strategy. That was the moment our team was forged. Once we had broken down that barrier, we were able to create an honest, constructive dynamic that has propelled us forward ever since.

One thing that sets great teams apart is when each person levels up the people around them. They improve the performance by raising the bar, giving feedback, and asking for more. When you choose to join or form a team, ask yourself about the people you would be working with: Are they generative and generous, or are they selfish and destructive? Are they focused on mutual growth or individual success? Are they focused on the customer or on personal recognition? Note that these qualities aren't necessarily fixed in a person. They are shaped by circumstances and what kinds of behavior are rewarded. Seek to find a team and a company where you can succeed together, where you can make those around you better, and you, in turn, will get better as well.

If you're on a good team, they have your back, no matter the circumstances. One day at Facebook I met with the CEO of a company we were considering acquiring. We were introduced as he walked into the room, and I sat down in the middle of a long table, as was my habit. The CEO sat at the head of the table. P.J. Linarducci, the product lead on my team who reported to me, sat on the other side, directly across from me.

The CEO began presenting about his company, and I noticed that he spoke directly to P.J., never once looking at me. I sat there without saying a word for the twenty-minute presentation, unsure what to do. Finally, P.J. looked at the CEO and said, "She actually decides if we buy your company, not me." The CEO looked horrified at the faux pas and stumbled over his apology. P.J. exemplified what it meant to be an ally, someone who was willing to step up and make things right, even when I was reluctant to.

These stories are widely shared among women in the workplace, especially in male-dominated environments. One product manager, Alexa Krakaris, shared a note that went viral within Facebook about how she attended SIGGRAPH, a large conference on computer graphics, and was completely ignored. Once she made her teammate, Ittai Barzilay, aware of it, he used his influence to bring her into the conversation and call out those who repeatedly ignored her. In the comments, women—both junior and senior—shared their recollections of how their teammates helped call out this kind of behavior and stepped up to give them authority. For women leaders, their teams would declare, "She is the head of X," or, "I work on her team" as a way of giving them power.

At Facebook, many on the technology side, such as engineers, product managers, designers, data scientists, and researchers, enter the company as generalists. They pick their teams once they are in boot camp. Many of them face the question of how to choose among all the options. My advice? Pick your manager, then your team, and then your product. Your manager will be your first mentor and potentially your sponsor. Your team is who you will spend nearly all your work hours with, and your product will be better if you build it with a group of people you love.

Each of the teams I have worked with has been a part of my life for years. You will work on many projects in your career, but the people you work with and the relationships you build are what you will take with you. Optimize for people and the rest will follow.

---

circle

|'sərk(ə)l|

noun

a group of people with shared professions, interests, or acquaintances[14]

Finding Belonging

A circle is complete, a whole. A circle at work is a close-knit group with shared interests that offers mutual support. Your circle is where you find belonging, a group in which you can be yourself.

This informal allyship network is what makes it possible for us to do what we do. We had a Lean In Circle at Facebook called Leading Ladies, made up of women VPs from across the company. This group of women supported and bolstered one another through hardships, difficult career decisions, and challenges at home. Through reorganizations, setbacks, and even eventual departures, these women were each other's cheering sections and shoulders to cry on. When I left the company, this group sent me a silver bracelet with tiny bamboo-shaped beads to remind me that women are strong yet flexible. Bamboo has more tensile strength than steel and serves as scaffolding for building Hong Kong skyscrapers. We were each other's scaffolding even in the hardest of times, and that was how we were able to scale new heights. I wear their gift every day to remind myself of this special group of women who carried me forward in my career.

Finding Your Circle

Magic happens when you have a group of friends and colleagues who have your back. They root for you, listen to your troubles, and encourage you to pick yourself up and try again. These are the people who you call on when you are struggling, and they are the friends who celebrate with you during times of joy. A group like this is where you hear the hard truths and challenge one another to be your best selves.

Your circle is your support system. These groups foster connection, even among introverts like me, and remind us how important mutual support can be. I have been fortunate to be a part of several of these groups over the years.

Abigail Wen, the *New York Times* bestselling author who spent ten years writing before getting her first novel published, found her circle among her critique partners. When she was ready to give up on herself, they kept her going. "I hit a low point when my fifth novel was turned down," she explained. "They picked me back up and put me on my feet again. They encouraged me, telling me my writing was good and publishable and that there were systemic and other reasons why it wasn't getting through. I was able to keep going, revised my manuscript on draft twenty-seven, and *Loveboat, Taipei* went on to sell at auction, publish with HarperCollins, and hit the *New York Times* list. I would not have this book in the world today without them."

Circles can be organically or artificially created, but the most important thing is that everyone has the full trust and support of everyone else. You can create your circle through work, online groups, social activities, or professional communities. The critical factor is that you feel safe enough in the group to be yourself and that you can receive and give support. Knowing that you have a group of people who can catch you if you fall means you can fly higher and push harder than you could alone.

Every success story is not one of an individual working alone but of someone who had allies standing alongside them, lifting them up, and carrying them forward through adversity.

The narrative of your career will be filled with twists and turns, triumphs and failures. But the one thing you will carry with you is the people you meet and the relationships you build. They will be the hands that comfort you when you face hardship and pull you up to the next plateau as you climb onward and upward.

Your journey is made with the support of your allies—your mentors, your sponsors, your team, and your circle. Having them by your side will take you farther than you can imagine.

RULE #7

Embrace Who
You Are

*The most important relationship in life is the one we
have with ourselves.*

—Diane von Furstenberg

D on't be bossy."
　　"Be ladylike."
"Don't be too loud."
"Don't be difficult."

We teach girls not to stand out too much, not to take up too
much space. We train our daughters to conform from an early age.
Subtle hints abound, from what appears on onesies, like "Pretty like
mommy, smart like daddy," to video games where the silent male
hero saves the princess. We inundate girls with traditional Disney
princesses like Aurora, Snow White, Cinderella, or Ariel, all waiting
for a prince to save them. Aurora slept through *Sleeping Beauty*, while
Snow White needed a prince to awaken her. In *The Little Mermaid*,

Ariel quite literally gives up her voice to be with a man who doesn't even recognize her. Marvel put out twenty superhero movies over twenty years, all with male leads, before *Captain Marvel* came out (nineteen if you count the second billing of the Wasp in *Ant-Man and the Wasp*).[1] Only in the past few years have women been allowed to be heroes in their own right.

Overwhelmingly in the media, men are heroes and women are catalysts or supporting figures, not leaders. My daughters complain that every video game we play together has a boy as a hero. When we played *The Legend of Zelda: Breath of the Wild*, my daughter Bethany complained that it was unfair that the game starred Link, who got to rest for a century, while Princess Zelda held off Calamity Ganon, the dark, destructive force that destroyed her kingdom. From *Xenoblade Chronicles* to *The Witcher* to *Halo*, all of which we played as a family, the vast majority of popular video games allow you to inhabit the role of a male hero with supporting female companions.

I rebelled against the princess phase when my girls were young because I objected to that message. I wanted my girls to write their own stories, not be mere players in someone else's. I fed their Hello Kitty craze instead, until my sister brought them Hello Kitty princess dresses and I was sunk. Frustrated with the messages about a woman's role, I bought my girls T-shirts with a quote from Sheryl Sandberg: "Pretty like daddy, smart like mommy."[2]

The Lessons We Are Taught

Women are taught to change who they are to fit into a standard. From a young age, girls are expected to conform to specific norms. Teachers invest more time teaching boys and praise them more than girls. They interrupt girls more and make more space for boys to speak in the classroom.[3] In a 2015 study, math tests graded by teachers showed bias toward those with boys' names versus those with girls' names, but no such bias appeared when the tests were graded blindly.[4] This led to more boys from those cohorts of children later entering the STEM field. Another study, published in *Educational Researcher* in 2020, showed that while teachers graded the tests fairly, they subsequently rated the abilities of boys much higher than the abilities of girls. They especially punished girls of color in math, even when their test scores were similar. This study randomized the names shown to the teachers, highlighting the insidious effect of gender bias, even among those who educate the next generation.[5]

At work, managers give men more direct coaching and feedback, which leads to faster career development and growth.[6] Society signals that some fields are not for women, particularly STEM. When women get to the workforce, we are given feedback that we are emotional or "abrasive."[7] When we deviate from society's standards of behavior, we're described as bossy or sassy and called prima donnas, while boys are praised for being assertive and for leading.

The world is full of signals telling women that we aren't good enough, that our ideas aren't worth listening to, that we are lesser. A lifetime of slowly being pushed aside teaches us to distrust our instincts and suppress our points of view. We are taught that complaining makes us difficult and that being ambitious makes us unlikeable. But each of us, as my friend and coach Sanyin Siang says, has a "superpower" that makes us special and unique, and that's something no one can take away. Learning to identify, understand, and embrace that superpower is how we can achieve more than we could ever have imagined.

Finding Your Superpower

For a long time I struggled with trusting myself and what I saw. I didn't think there was anything special about me because many people could do what I did. Because I grew up being so different from everyone around me, I sat back as an observer, careful not to say the wrong thing or to stand out. But that also taught me not to trust my gut or share my point of view. I thought that if no one else could see my perspective, then it wasn't valid.

When I joined Facebook eleven years ago, Sheryl Sandberg was the one who interviewed me. I told her that we should build social commerce—a marketplace—on Facebook. I could tell she wasn't crazy about the idea, but she was gracious. For five more years, despite my reluctance to make waves, I kept pitching the idea. I could see all these moms trading on Facebook in mom groups, and I overcame my introversion to advocate for us to build the product to enable this feature for everyone. I would constantly talk to the other executives and point out that people were already buying and selling on the platform. At one point, the chief product officer, Chris Cox, looked at me quizzically and said, "Why would anyone buy things on Facebook?" I could see this entire community of people who were trying to do commerce on Facebook using groups. And nobody else was paying attention to it.

Then I started working with a coach, Katia Verresen. For a long time I'd tell her about something I noticed, but then follow up with, "If no one else sees it, then maybe I'm wrong!"

She would say, "Or maybe you're right, and they just can't see it. You need to trust yourself."

We often talk ourselves down or out of something—something that's unique to us—because it would make us stand out too much. It makes us uncomfortable to be different, to amplify what sets us apart.

During one of my sessions with Katia, I said, "I wish people could see what I see." I have noticed that many times in my career, the answer seemed obvious, but I feared speaking up because if I was the only person who could see it, then I was probably wrong.

She replied, "That's it. That's your superpower." At first I didn't believe her. I wasn't ever able to convince people of what I could see. But she said that my ability to see what others couldn't, to connect the dots that others couldn't connect, was what made me special. She encouraged me to leverage my insights rather than suppress them.

When I joined Facebook, I was one of the few moms at the company. For years I was the only mom in the product management organization, where many of the new products were germinated. Because I lived a different life than most others, I was able to leverage parts of the network that they couldn't see. Eventually, I decided that if Facebook would not build commerce, I would leave to pursue it. I had already arranged backing and a cofounder when my manager looked at my list of new products, pointed to commerce, and said, "What about bringing that to Mark?" I was stunned. A couple of weeks later, I pitched to Mark building Facebook Marketplace, a product that now has over a billion monthly active users.

Don't Allow External Things to Define You

We are often defined by things outside ourselves. Our identities are set early on based on what happens to us. But we get to decide whether to embrace or reject the labels others put on us. I allowed growing up different from everyone around me to turn me into someone who was "the other," and I tried to compensate. My difference, and my desire to hide it, defined me for so long that I didn't know how to take off that cloak. It felt so much a part of me that I convinced myself that it was inherent to who I was.

I was the odd one out, the girl who never quite belonged, and this identity became as ingrained in me as my hair or eye color. When I got to Stanford Graduate School of Business, I took the well-known "Touchy Feely" class, and there, my fellow students reinforced how I felt about myself. Touchy Feely is a class called Interpersonal Dynamics, and it has been the most popular elective at Stanford for forty-five years.[8] Students are split up into groups of twelve called T-Groups. These groups meet for a minimum of three hours a week for the quarter and then go on a multiday retreat together where everyone shares how they feel about one another based on their perception of their teammates' behavior.[9] As a quiet, Chinese American Christian, I was told how I seemed different, foreign somehow. These were people who came from different circumstances, countries, and backgrounds, and they nearly all had the same feedback: that I held back from others and had trouble connecting and opening up.

That was when I realized that the foreignness I had grown up with was no longer imposed on me by others. Rather, it was something I had begun to inhabit by choice. I had allowed others to define me so extensively that I lived by their definition well beyond the time it was true. That lesson stuck with me as I left Stanford for the workforce, but it took me years to unravel that cloak. I allowed others to wall me in, and then I used those stones to build a fortress I could inhabit. Taking the pieces down stone by stone enabled me to open up and connect with people.

I'm not the only one who has had to struggle not to be defined by others. Sylvia Acevedo has served as the CEO of the Girl Scouts of the USA, the chair of President Obama's Initiative on Educational Excellence for Hispanics in Early Education, and a board member of Qualcomm, a Fortune 500 company focused on wireless technology. *Forbes* named her as one of "America's Top 50 Women in Tech." When asked about the key to her long and impactful career, Sylvia said, "I refuse to be defined by the rules of others." Growing up in the modest community of Las Cruces, New Mexico, Sylvia was born in the 1950s, the child of a Mexican-born mother with an eighth-grade-level education and a Mexican American scientist father. When Sylvia was a little girl, her sister Laura was struck by a bout of meningitis that left her disabled. Sylvia sought refuge in the Girl Scouts, ultimately gaining the confidence and skills to take her far beyond her modest hometown.

Sylvia's superpower was that she believed she could do anything regardless of what was written on paper. As a woman, she entered STEM at a time when few like her sought after those opportunities, but she embraced the challenge. After graduating from New Mexico State University, she joined NASA's *Voyager 2* team. From there, she went back to get her master's engineering degree from Stanford University, making her one of the first Hispanic women or men to do so. Then she went to work for IBM as an engineer. "I didn't accept labels. I told myself I belonged, and I made sure I did," she said of her journey.

Then, when she was twenty-eight, a tragedy changed her life and nearly took her off-track. Her father, who had struggled with mental health and control issues for many years, killed her mother and committed suicide. Devastated, Sylvia took over care for her disabled sister along with her aunt's family while she struggled to overcome the mark the tragedy had placed on her life. Over the years, she worked through the negative patterns she had learned from her parents. "I had to overcome the shame. I had to find forgiveness to achieve freedom."

Sylvia moved forward from that tragedy and went on to work at various big-name tech companies, including Dell, Autodesk, and

Apple, never allowing others to underestimate her. When she was told she couldn't be a leader as a woman in Latin America, she traveled to Chile and got business leaders to write her letters of recommendation. When she wanted to lead a business in Asia, she was told that a Hispanic woman would not be accepted there, so she went to Hong Kong and Macao and got references to prove that she could. Both times, she defied the odds and never allowed "can't" to enter her mind.

A mentor at Dell once told Sylvia, "Stop going to the hardware store looking for milk," and she took it to heart. Sylvia pushed herself to seek new opportunities and ways to learn and grow. When she felt blocked, she found another way, but she never stayed where there wasn't a path forward.

Eventually, her path led to where her impact could bring her full circle. Sylvia served on the Girl Scouts board from 2009 to 2016, when she was called on by her fellow board members to serve as the CEO. Leveraging her knowledge of business and engineering processes, along with her passion for the Girl Scouts, she remade the century-old organization. During her four-year tenure, she created 146 new programs centered on entrepreneurship, the outdoors, civic engagement, STEM, and even cyber skills. Thanks to her work, girls from across America earned over one million STEM badges, inspiring another generation of girls just as Sylvia was inspired during a time of tragedy.

Amplifying Your Superpower

When I was a child, I used to go to my mom's jewelry box every few months and take out her necklaces and bracelets to untangle. She threw everything in there, not caring that they would turn into a single tangle of gold, the strands intertwined so tightly that they became an indistinguishable mass. I remember that feeling I had of taking something that looked like an impossible jumble of precious jewelry and slowly and methodically unraveling it one strand at a time. I would follow the threads and loops, tracing them to their origins, spending satisfying hours taking something unusable and returning it to its original form.

I love assembling puzzles, understanding hard problems, and working on complex strategies. The same thrill I had as a child, I still get from solving problems, whether at work or at home. One day I encountered an insight that no one in the tech industry talked about. I didn't know what to do with it. For four years, I sat on it, mulling it over, worried that it was only my imagination. I spoke to dozens of women and even wrote a full report on it, but I couldn't bring myself to publish it because I didn't trust my intuition.

At first blush, the problem appeared trivial and not worth exploring. When I started my career in product management in 2002, the field was gender balanced. Amy Klement was the vice president of product at PayPal while Judy Kirkpatrick held the same role at eBay. Many of the managers and directors of both companies were women. At one point, at Amy's leadership table, the head of each of the major product teams was a woman, and the group had a 50-50 gender balance.

Seven years later, when I went to Facebook, I couldn't even get a job there in product management. When I was later invited into the product group, there were only three other women product managers, and we made up less than 10 percent of the organization.

Product management is an important but relatively small area in technology companies. In total, there may be a hundred thousand or so practitioners. But these product managers are the people who set the strategy to address the problems tech companies across the world are prioritizing. They write the road maps and lead the execution behind your favorite product experiences, both hardware and software. Who product managers are and how diverse the field is matters because they determine where billions of dollars of technology research and development go each year. They pitch new products, determining what problems are addressed and which issues are left behind. Many product leaders go on to become tech advisors, investors, founders, board members, and CEOs, continuing to amplify their impact.

Somehow, between when I started in product in 2002 and when I left eBay in 2009, the field went from one with gender equality to one that was extremely unbalanced. Many women product managers couldn't get hired at other companies. Some stayed in their companies and advanced, but many moved laterally to other functions or left the field altogether.

No one talked about this issue openly, but behind closed doors, the women PMs of Facebook noticed. I decided to partner with Ruta Singh, the head of recruiting. We started by unpacking the reasons there were so few women and began systematically fixing the issue. For years we worked on moving the numbers from under 10 percent to parity, and it took real work. But the question that still tugged at the back of my mind was, "What changed?"

I stumbled upon the answer to the mystery when I chatted with April Underwood, then the VP of product at Slack. On that call, she shared how she had been a product manager on a gender-balanced team at Travelocity but ended up going to Google as a partner technology manager because she lacked a computer science degree. This was even though she had been an engineer previously.

That conversation sparked something in me. Part of the work we had done at Facebook to improve diversity was to remove the computer science degree requirement. Then we removed the technical interview. We did this because the three most senior and successful women product managers in the company, Fidji Simo, Naomi Gleit, and I, did not even qualify to interview for our own roles because we lacked the degree requirement. We had all come in through other roles, only to be later invited into the exclusive product club, the gateway for many of the senior leaders in the company.

I sought out well-respected product managers from across the industry and asked them what happened. I came upon a former Google product manager who told me that around 2004, the company had changed its requirements for PMs. Engineers had complained that the PMs were not technical enough, so they added the requirement of the CS degree. At the time, Google was the vanguard of the tech industry, as it is now. Many companies followed its example. In 2005 and the years since, women have earned about one in five computer science degrees.[10]

As a result, the new classes of product managers became more and more male-dominated. Even women who had successful product management careers at other companies, including me, could no longer change companies as PMs, and instead were forced to take on other roles.

I spent years fixing this through my work as the PM lead for recruiting at Facebook. I started by interviewing every woman who applied for a PM job at the company. We started hosting events and dinners for women to show them that women leaders did exist at the company. Progress was slow because we required at least some PM experience, and many women couldn't even get their first job coming out of school if they didn't have the computer science degree.

Four years after speaking to April, I pushed myself to publish my findings in 2020 in an article on LinkedIn titled "What Happened to Women in Product?"[11] The reaction in our industry was incredible.

Dozens of women told me that the same thing had happened to them, and they had felt like it was just them—that they were not good enough and that was why they became stuck.

I saw something no one else saw, and for years I was too afraid to say anything. I had invested seven years in changing Facebook's hiring practices and processes to help us get to gender equality, yet I couldn't quite allow myself to share what I had noticed because I didn't trust myself to be right.

I decided after publishing that article that I would no longer hold back. I would openly put my ideas out there to be discussed and criticized rather than sitting on them and holding them back. A few months later, I started the new year of 2021 with a newsletter in which I write something every week that I observe, good or bad. No more waiting for years or keeping thoughts to myself. Instead, I want to push myself to embrace what I see and share it with others.

Embracing Your Magic

Much of what women are taught to do is suppress what makes us different, to fix the things about us that stand out too much or draw too much attention. In the field of technology, Fidji never fails to stand out. In a world of hoodies, jeans, and sneakers, Fidji commands the room with four-inch heels, a couture dress, and perfect makeup, even on her worst days. And she's had many of those due to her health, but she never lets that slow her down.

As the head of the Facebook app, Fidji Simo ran the most popular app in the world. Her decisions touched the lives of 2.5 billion monthly users. She rose through the ranks of the Facebook organization from a junior product marketing role to product management to product group lead and went on to become one of the company's youngest vice presidents. In March 2019 Mark Zuckerberg asked her to take the helm of the product he had created from his dorm room, placing in her hands the eponymous crown jewel of the company.

Fidji was born and grew up in Sète, a town in the south of France with fewer than fifty thousand residents. Every man in her family fished for a living, and her mother owned a clothing boutique. One day she saw a woman on television pursuing a career in business, and Fidji decided then and there to emulate her. She recalls telling her mother, "One day I am going to be an executive, have a suitcase, and rush through an airport." Though her parents and generations of her family lived in Sète, they encouraged her to follow her dream. That led her to pursue her education and become the first person in her family to graduate from high school and go on to college.

Though her path was difficult, Fidji never wavered in her belief that anything was possible. After college she went on to business school, where she had a chance to spend a semester at the University of California, Los Angeles (UCLA), and fell in love with the US. She immediately picked up her life and moved here, joining eBay on the strategy team and starting her career in tech.

In 2011 Fidji joined Facebook, then a company with fewer than three thousand employees, in product marketing. Her true passion was building, so she carved a path to move over to product management at a time when Facebook still required a technical degree for the role. She rose through the ranks as an innovator, driving much of Facebook's monetization strategy on mobile and developing major products in entertainment, including Facebook Watch and Facebook Live. She also incubated the teams focused on news, civic engagement, and creator monetization, and fostered the games product in the pivot to livestreaming. One of the fastest-growing leaders in the company, Fidji joined Mark's small executive team in 2017.

Fidji's grit and belief in what made her different got her through obstacle after obstacle. When Watch first launched, it struggled to gain traction. Fidji listened as the company debated killing the product shortly after launch. She had bet her career and reputation on making this billion-dollar investment successful, and she watched as issues and doubts plagued the product. She recalls, "My mom reminded me that the odds of a fisherman's daughter from a small town in France becoming a Facebook exec in the US had been slim. But I had never focused on the odds, always on taking one step after another along the path to get to my destination. So that's what I did: I reconnected to my excitement for this vision, cleared all the energy of the nonbelievers out of my space, and kept iterating on the product, one feature at a time, until it turned into a major success."

The success of Facebook Live sent Fidji's career into overdrive, winning her accolades both from the entertainment industry and internally at Facebook. During that time of tremendous career growth, Fidji became pregnant with her daughter, Willow. Due to complications from endometriosis, she was placed on bed rest for six months, all while leading some of the most important initiatives in the company and a four-hundred-person team.

Having always relied on her hard work and preparation to will products to life, Fidji lost the ability to lead her team in person. The medication that was saving her baby threatened Fidji's life, but she knew she wanted to give Willow the best chance possible. She took a step back and remained on restrictive bed rest, all while leading her team from afar and learning to delegate and scale. Fidji also did something she had not allowed herself to do before: lead with vulnerability. She had always out-planned and out-prepared everyone, and learning to delegate required her to share her situation and rely on others to bring her vision to life. This experience made her realize that vulnerability helped her build stronger bonds with her team, without losing any of her hard-earned credibility.

When faced with each challenge, Fidji adapted and evolved. While she still led, she had to learn to change tack as she suffered from a chronic condition. Even as she struggled through tests and surgeries, she grew the Facebook app to 2.5 billion users and added dozens of new products and features. Through her bed rest and her battle with endometriosis and eventually with an autonomic nervous system disorder called POTS, Fidji didn't allow her pain to stop her, even if it meant using a wheelchair to make it to the stage to interview Diane von Furstenberg at the Women in Product conference keynote or hosting strategy reviews while reclining when POTS dropped her blood pressure. She learned to lead with openness about her health from a place of strength and confidence to inspire anyone to pursue their dreams despite the challenges thrown their way.

Fidji's superpower is that she believes in the magic of the possible, and she has dedicated herself to paying it forward by finding the magic in others. Four years ago I went to her office after I had been passed over for a job after a major company reshuffle at Facebook. She looked me directly in the eye and said, "Deb, we both know you will be a CEO someday." When the chance came for me to lead Ancestry, she encouraged me to stretch my wings and take the job. Fidji's superpower of finding the magic in others and amplifying it has changed the lives of many who have had the chance to meet her, including me.

In August 2021, the opportunity came for Fidji to take the helm of the $40 billion tech unicorn Instacart as the new CEO. The founder and CEO stepped aside to give her the reins as the company prepared to go public. Her magic will only continue to grow in her new role.

Take Charge of Your Story

Embracing what makes you unique means owning your individuality rather than conforming to the expectations of others. Amplifying your personal superpower is being unafraid to be different and not allowing yourself to be defined by the rules of others. Your history, family story, and experiences are all part of who you are. You can choose to embrace or reject that story, but it is woven deep into you from your birth. You can live your life reacting to it and being a victim of it, or you can leverage it as your motivation and inspiration.

"What made me who I am is in my DNA, and that DNA reflects the woman I became," said Diane von Furstenberg, creator of the iconic wrap dress and her eponymous brand. Eighteen months before she was born, her mother, Liliane Nahmias, was one of six million Jews the Nazis imprisoned. At age twenty-two, Liliane was liberated from Auschwitz weighing only forty-nine pounds, barely alive. She returned to her home in Belgium, where Diane's grandmother carefully fed and cared for her until her health was largely restored. Diane's mother later married, but the doctor warned her not to have children for three years due to the risk of death for her and her unborn child. Nine months later, Diane was born.

"Knowing that my mother wasn't supposed to survive, the minute I was born, I had already won," Diane says. "That explains everything about my life. Everything after was not as big of a gift as that." Diane's superpower was her sense of clarity about who she was and what she wanted to be. She wanted to be a woman in charge—in charge of her life, her work, and her legacy.

One day Diane met a man in Italy at a printing factory who taught her about knits, color, and fabrics. Her mother then helped her get a ticket to New York, where she realized her calling. She went back to that factory and asked the man to make some samples so she could showcase them in America. Returning to America, she started her company, Diane von Furstenberg, focused on giving women the affordable and beautiful wrap dress. Then-editor of *Vogue* Diana Vreeland loved the designs and featured them, putting Diane's brand on the map.

For the past several decades, Diane has leveraged her super-power to help other women to feel in charge and take control of their own lives. She built her company and brand while living life on her own terms. Despite two battles with cancer, she has continued to live her truth and pass her self-assuredness on to women through her designs. Her simple and elegant wrap dress is an iconic reminder of the power of women to live their confidence.

Around her neck, Diane wears a gold pendant with script in her handwriting that reads, "InCharge." Just like the wrap dress, it reflects the inspiration she has been to countless women.

What makes us women special often feels ill-fitting or uncomfortable, precisely because it is unusual or rare. We look around and feel the urge to conform, to stifle our voices and seek safety. But our super-power is what makes each of us unique, which is precisely why we should cultivate it and invest in it. It gives us something someone else doesn't have, whether it's Sylvia's ability to belong anywhere, Fidji's faith in her magic and that of others, or Diane's ability to pass her confidence and passion on to the women of the working world.

Embracing who we are means we can take the power we were gifted with and use it to make an impact. Something inside you is yours alone, something you see or feel that others can't. Don't hide that light. Instead, let it shine brightly, and show others the way forward.

Create Balance
at Home

The most important career choice you'll make is who
you marry.

—SHERYL SANDBERG

I met my husband when I was eighteen. It was my first weekend as a freshman at Duke, and a childhood friend of mine invited me to his church, where he introduced me to David.

At the time, David was a senior at the University of North Carolina at Chapel Hill. He was dressed in a pinstripe suit and yellow tie. That combined with his irreverent and flippant sense of humor caused me to have an immediate visceral negative reaction to him. These emotions continued for most of my freshman year. Needless to say, our path to marriage was not an easy one, and we learned that love doesn't always conquer all obstacles. We had to create the kind of partnership we would one day want. Five years of dating— half of which were long-distance—twenty years of marriage, three kids, and four moves later, we have learned the lessons of how to have a successful marriage that supports two careers and a family.

Taking back your power in the workplace means not working the second shift. *The Second Shift*, a book published in 1989 by Arlie Russell Hochschild, describes the household responsibilities that remain after the work day.[1] What happens at home affects your success as much as—if not more than—what happens at work. The difference between a partner who supports your career and one who does not is enormous.

Plan Your Marriage Like You Plan Your Wedding

Relationships can affect your long-term career potential. The single decision to date and marry someone who supports your dreams can change the course of your life. It reverberates through every day, in both big and small ways.

While David and I were dating, we attended a marriage seminar and took a detailed survey about our expectations around marriage. We had been in a relationship for three years by this point, but that survey forced us to confront hidden preconceptions we had brought into our partnership, which would naturally extend to our marriage. Though we had a great deal in common, basic assumptions about how our household would work were just that: assumptions. We had never talked about them. It was sobering to realize I had done more comprehensive surveys to get matched with my college roommate than I had to select a life partner. Seeing the answers in black and white forced both of us to discuss our deeply held beliefs about the reality of what our marriage would look like.

While we had grown up in similar families in some ways, our

parents were completely different. David's father was the dom-
inant force in the family, whereas my mother was the household
leader. David had always assumed he would take on the traditional
breadwinner role and be the primary decision maker. I defaulted
to assuming our marriage would be more similar to my parents',
where my mother had the final say. Our conversation about our roles
opened our eyes to the major challenges we would face together,
but it also brought us to a much better understanding of our own
assumptions. It also revealed the roots of many of our seemingly
mundane disagreements.

Couples in America, on average, spend nearly $34,000 on their
weddings. In many places, this is almost half their annual household income.[2] They are engaged, on average, for about thirteen and
a half months.[3] How much of that time spent planning the wedding do couples spend discussing how their marriage will work?
In our society, we celebrate weddings with months, if not years, of
planning—all for one day. What if we planned and prepared for marriage the same way? We spend weeks on things like the perfect cake,
how the bouquets will look, and music choices for the first dance.
Imagine if we spent an equal amount of time discussing how we
would merge our finances and support each other's careers.

Little girls grow up dreaming of weddings, but not of the reality
of marriage. One becomes a long distant memory, however, while
the other can change the entire course of our future.

From the Wedding to the Second Shift

Success in the workplace for women starts at home. Imagine two
women, each with two children and in the middle of her career.
Each is married to an equally successful spouse. One woman has a

husband who takes on half the household management and half the cognitive load of child-rearing. The other woman goes home to work the entirety of the "second shift," managing dinner, juggling the kids' schedules, and handling chores. Which woman has a lighter mental load and support to focus on her career?

This extra load is a genuine issue. The Bureau of Labor Statistics' American Time Use Survey shows that, on average, women spend over two hours per day more than men doing housework and child-care, 5.7 hours per day versus 3.6.[4] Even among couples in which both partners work at least thirty-five hours per week, women still work an hour more at home than their male counterparts. This is largely because of the way gender roles are set up. Women take on everyday chores, such as cooking and cleaning, whereas men take on less frequent chores, such as taking out the trash and mowing the yard.

This disparity in household responsibilities starts at the beginning of a relationship, but children further exacerbate the inequity. Mothers with children under six reduce their work hours as they ramp up their home responsibilities, but fathers don't. This means mothers have less time at work, usually during a period when they are moving into management.[5] Some have speculated that perhaps women are not as ambitious, but this is not borne out by the data. In a survey of two hundred thousand people in the workforce, women and men exhibited equal levels of ambition, but women ran into more barriers as their careers progressed.[6] It's not that women lack ambition; it's that the combination of pressures at home and at work saps it from them.

The second shift holds women back in many ways. Studies of six Western countries showed that in all cases, women took significant pay cuts after having children. In the US, the long-term difference is a persistent 30 percent difference in earnings.[7]

In her seminal 2012 *Atlantic* article, "Why Women Still Can't Have It All," Anne-Marie Slaughter gave voice to the ambivalence that many professional women feel. We have built a society where women face substantial barriers in the workplace, and an important ingredient for success is a supportive partner. "I could never have had the career I have had without my husband, Andrew Moravcsik, who is a tenured professor of politics and international affairs at Princeton," she wrote.[8] Although having the support of a partner is only part of the equation (Slaughter highlighted that women still face structural challenges), it's undeniably vital. Imagine attempting to have a career that requires global travel—or any travel—without it.

Three years after the publication of Anne-Marie's article, her husband, Andrew, returned to the pages of the *Atlantic* with the article "Why I Put My Wife's Career First." In it, he discusses how he became what he calls the "lead parent," enabling his wife to succeed outside the home.[9] These articles highlight a reality that we often gloss over: home life is not a realm separate from work. For both women and men, it can be either an inhibitor or an enabler of success.

Children as the Great Chasm

David and I had a balanced partnership before the birth of our first child. We had been married for nearly five years, during which we grew our careers in Silicon Valley. But even in the most balanced marriages, children challenge all the assumptions about the relationship.

Before we had kids, my husband had never changed a diaper. And he had barely spent any time with children, let alone babies. As an only child, he wanted kids more badly than I did, and I was skeptical. We had a full partnership in our marriage. We split the work equally, supported each other emotionally, and never let the brunt of the home upkeep fall too much to either of us. Still, I worried that he would not step up in fatherhood and that we would fall into the dynamic of the traditional marriages our parents had.

This was not a theoretical concern. According to a 2017 Bright Horizons survey, 86 percent of working mothers say they "handle all family and household responsibilities." They are twice as likely to be running the day-to-day functions of the household and three times as likely to be taking care of their children's schedules. Even women who are the primary breadwinners are three times more likely to be running their households than breadwinning husbands.[10] These stats gave me pause as I faced impending motherhood. No matter how egalitarian a partnership David and I had, we faced the possibility that parenthood would upset that balance.

Jonathan was born in 2006 after a stressful pregnancy, and David was immediately in love. While I was waiting for the epidural to wear off, the nurse came in to show David how to change a diaper. I thought he would balk, but David carefully paid attention and changed his first diaper before commenting, "It is amazing they let us do this even though we have no idea what we are doing."

During our hospital stay, David would stand over the newborn crib, stare down at Jonathan, and whisper, "He is the cutest baby in the world."

I would respond, "I am pretty sure that other parents wouldn't agree."

David would reply, "Well, they would be wrong."

Smitten as we were, we soon noticed that something was not quite right with Jonathan. He struggled to breastfeed, cried uncontrollably for hours, and threw up copious amounts of milk after each feeding. This endless cycle of feeding, crying, and vomiting ended with both Jonathan and I in tears. We had moved from an equal marriage into something unknown and scary. I could barely make it through the day on so little sleep with a baby I couldn't soothe. And with each speed bump, my anxiety grew.

It was during this stressful period that David surprised me. I remember him saying to me, "You take care of what goes into the baby, and I will take care of what comes out." And he stuck to it. He ended up changing 90 percent of the diapers for all three of our children, never once wavering from that commitment. When Jonathan was later diagnosed with a type of baby reflux that made it hard for him to nurse and keep down milk, David took the pumped breast milk and fed him at all hours. He later did the same for our youngest, and he still jokes that those two kids prefer him to me because all babies know where their milk comes from: Daddy, of course.

I would like to think my husband is extraordinary, and he is in many ways, but the nature of our relationship is also different because we set out to make it that way.

A lot of the imbalance in marriages has to do with expectations that are set from the start. Once you fall into a pattern, it is more difficult to break free, so being intentional about how you set up your marriage is critical to how it evolves over your lifetime. Much of what couples do in marriage are patterns born of how they met and came together, expectations based on their parents, and unspoken habits they unknowingly fall into.

Household management is a task in itself. Some husbands ask, "Why don't you just ask me if you need something done?" But the process of keeping track of what needs to be done is a vast part of the mental load. In an egalitarian marriage, each spouse does their tasks independently and trusts that the other is doing their share. There is no asking—and certainly no pestering.

A Note on Nagging

Popular media often portrays women as nagging men to do work around the house. *Nagging* is a pejorative term for what some husbands expect wives to do: household management and task allocation. We live in a system where many women are placed in an impossible position: ask and remind and you are considered a nag, but not asking means taking on more work yourself. A marriage where this dynamic takes hold becomes toxic. If you ever fight with your partner about nagging, treat it not as a character flaw but as a symptom of a lack of clear expectations and alignment. Focus instead on the root of the issue: that one person is managing the other and that you have moved away from an equal partnership.

Old Habits Die Hard, So Don't Let Practices Turn into Old Habits

Before David went off to law school, he rarely did his own laundry. His parents got married when they were in their late thirties, and he was born over a month premature. Worried about another premature birth, his mother decided not to attempt to have another child. As a result, David's parents doted on him, going as far as to cook separate dinners for him because he didn't like to eat Chinese food. When he went off to college, he chose the University of North Carolina at Chapel Hill, not far from his childhood home. On weekends, he would return home and have his mom do his laundry.

While we were dating, I noticed little of this. We dated long distance for several years and didn't move in together until the week after we got married, when we relocated to California. One day, several months later, I went to visit my new in-laws with him. At our home, I did the laundry—often only when we were running out of clothes—but it always got done. David always carefully put his clothing in the hamper and put it away after I folded it, and I never noticed anything amiss. During this particular visit, I saw David drop his dirty laundry on the floor in a pile. His mom stopped by our room, picked it up, and took it to the washer like it was the most normal thing in the world. I thought it was an anomaly, but then it happened again: he left some clothes on the banister in the hallway, and they disappeared, only to reappear, washed and folded, in our suitcase.

I asked David what was going on, why he couldn't even be bothered to bring his clothes downstairs to the hamper. He replied, "Oh, I didn't even notice. I guess I just fell into old habits."

To reiterate, this was a Harvard-trained lawyer who went home, left his dirty laundry on the floor, and let his mother wash it for him—something he would never have even considered doing at home with me. This was the same partner who took care of most of the bills and did all our grocery shopping. I was baffled until I realized that what had changed was not him but rather his environment. The habits he had learned as a child were so deeply ingrained that he returned to them without even noticing.

This is a feature in all relationships. Whatever pattern you set up from the start becomes a well-worn path for the long term. When there is an upset to the relationship, such as a move to a new location, a new job, or the birth of your first child, the roles are rejiggered and reset. The dynamic can change, but these are also opportunities to renegotiate what isn't working for both of you.

Right after the birth of our second child, Bethany, our family was on vacation while I was on maternity leave. While away, I received an email from an old friend from my days at PayPal. He asked if I was interested in a role on a new team at a hot startup called Facebook. It had fewer than a thousand employees at the time, and everyone worked relentless hours, but they were doing exciting things.

During that trip we discussed what pursuing that job would mean for our family. After Jonathan, my oldest, was born, I began working part-time. My four-day work week meant I was primarily responsible for managing the household and the children's schedules. We both knew this had to change if I was going to take on a new role.

We spent a weekend replanning our responsibilities together. David took on the pickups and drop-offs, took over the bills, and resumed grocery shopping as he had early in our marriage. This revised division of labor meant I was free to move to a more challenging opportunity without guilt.

We Risk Allowing Criticism
to Reduce Balance

My husband is a dishwasher fanatic, but we had an agreement that one person would cook and the other would clean. Each time it was my turn to do the dishes, I always felt anxious. According to David, each load had to be completely full and perfectly set, with the dishes all facing the proper way. Having never grown up using a dishwasher, I went into our marriage as a relative newbie. David's judgment of how I loaded the dishwasher prompted me to wait until he was showering or on his computer before I did the chore because I didn't want to be criticized.

This is common in many marriages. If one person cares about something more—the cleanliness of the toilets, for example, or how a diaper is changed—they tend to obsess about it to the point where the other person gives up. Most women are home on leave in the earlier days of their newborns' lives, so they fall into routines. Most fathers, with less leave, are more passive participants during this period. This is how the pattern is set: wives end up planning and managing every aspect of the household, and husbands take a back seat. As these habits form, they create an imbalance in your relationship that can be hard to set right.

This imbalance is also true of many other aspects of the household. A 2019 study from a group of sociologists discovered that mothers who were married to men spent more time on housework than even single mothers.[11] The amount of time they spent taking care of their children was the same.

Think about that for a minute. Women who had partners of the opposite sex spend more time on household chores than women who raised their families alone. Women live with such deeply held expectations around hearth and home that they invest more time when married to a man than when running their household without a partner. Women need more support at home if they are to thrive at work.

Because I worked part-time for the first three years we had children, I ended up taking on the lion's share of the household management. Once I went back to full-time, however, we worked to return to a more equitable balance. But this is not true for most women. During maternity leave, women shoulder many of the responsibilities around the home and continue to do so even after returning to work. This can carry on for years.

The Swim Lane Marriage

Looking at the data can feel discouraging, especially for women who want to find a balance between their careers and their home lives.

Thankfully, there is a solution to the second shift: what I like to call a "swim lane marriage." The term *swim lane diagram* (referring to a flow chart that delineates who does what) comes from a 1990 book, *Improving Performance*, by Geary Rummler and Alan Brache.[12] This philosophy focuses not only on what needs to be done but also by whom and where responsibilities can break down.

A swim lane marriage is one in which a husband and wife each take on their share of the mental and physical load. Each person is solely accountable and responsible for their role in the household flow (their "swim lane"). This is not a panacea for all the challenges of married life, but it does give you a tool for dismantling the second shift.

This kind of intentional partnership requires a couple to clearly communicate their expectations, decide on a division of labor up front, and, just as importantly, to stick to it. You would never expect your peer or colleague to take on responsibility for your work and dictate how you do it. The same goes for a household; as a wife, you should not be solely responsible for managing your family's home life and delegating tasks. Instead, imagine a marriage where you and your partner have mutual trust and agreement. Decide up front what needs to be done and then divide and conquer—no reminders, no checking up on each other. This works only if you mutually agree to forfeit the right to criticize the when and the how.

In our household, my husband meticulously plans all the vacations, and I do all the packing and unpacking with the kids. These are our swim lanes. David does all the school registration, pickups, and drop-offs, and I manage our kids' medical needs, like prescriptions, doctor appointments, dentist visits, and optometry. He pays the bills, and I go through the mail. We split cooking 50-50, but he does all the grocery shopping, and I manage the kids who set and clear the table and load and empty the dishwasher. I fix anything in the house that breaks, and David addresses issues with the cars. We constantly renegotiate our swim lanes as our commitments ebb and flow, but never in a way that feels unfair to either of us.

A Note on Unbalanced Partnerships or Single Parents

Unfortunately, not every woman has the benefits of a swim lane marriage. Many women live in a reality where they don't have an equal partner or have no partner at all. As of 2016, a quarter of households with kids are headed by single moms and 7 percent by single fathers.[13] And of those in opposite-sex marriages, balance seems hard to achieve no matter who is the breadwinner: "As wives' economic dependence on their husbands increases, women tend to take on more housework. But the more economically dependent men are on their wives, the less housework they do. Even women with unemployed husbands spend considerably more time on household chores than their spouses."[14] This imbalance hit home even more saliently during the pandemic lockdown when schools abruptly closed and one-third of moms in the workforce cut their hours or quit altogether to take on more at home.[15]

It is easy to take your partner for granted. For the past several years, David has taken Danielle to school and picked her up. After she returned to the classroom after the COVID virtual schooling, he dropped her off at 7:45 a.m., picked her up at 2:30 p.m., made her a snack, and then drove her to Chinese school at 3:30 p.m. At 5:45 p.m., he would pick her up and bring her home. Though he never complained about making twenty trips a week like this, he spent over an hour and a half each day shuttling her back and forth. At one point he was away for work for several days and handed these duties to me. Though I thought I had previously appreciated the complexity of arranging his work calendar to make this schedule work, it wasn't until it became my full responsibility that I truly understood how much effort it took.

One way to find more balance in your relationship is to try swapping duties for a month to gain a new perspective. This kind of empathy-building is the first and best step to create a more equal partnership. If your partner fails to do their part, let the work languish instead of jumping in to take over. This may be challenging, but it can help to illustrate what juggling your responsibilities is like and may open your partner's eyes to imbalances that they haven't yet noticed. At times, just seeing the inequitable balance of duties is the wake-up call needed to make a change or redistribute the tasks.

Another way is to find pivot points, moments when your life is up for renegotiation. One day the director of marketing for my team at Facebook, Neha Jogani, came to tell me she was quitting her job to stay home with her kids after multiple thorny childcare issues. I knew how much she loved her job, but I could see how she was burning out from juggling a demanding job with limited flexibility and an insecure childcare situation with two young kids. She said at the time, "I have no choice. I need to put my family first right now."

I begged her to consider returning to the workforce someday when the situation changed and advised her not to allow this to derail her career since I knew she could one day reach the C-suite. Her husband worked as an investor and, at that time in their marriage, was frequently away from home. Though they had a loving marriage, his demanding schedule meant she had to be the lead— and sometimes only—parent at home. Neha left a demanding role at the peak of her career and forged her path. To stay professionally relevant, she volunteered at a nonprofit, consulted for a range of companies, and joined two boards. This allowed her to have flexibility, prioritize her kids, and have a third child during those pivotal years when her husband traveled extensively.

During the pandemic lockdown, Neha went through a transition. Her husband worked from home, and for the first time since the kids were born, he internalized how much she put into making their household run. The lack of travel enabled him to be present with the family and find new ways to partner with Neha. At the same time, the pandemic made it possible for people in leadership roles to work remotely, something that was previously not an option. This turning point enabled Neha to get back into a demanding operating role, and today she is the VP of marketing at Roblox. This new role couldn't have happened without the upending of their lives by the pandemic, which enabled a renegotiation of their roles as partners.

I wish I could say there was a silver bullet to change unbalanced relationships, but there isn't a miracle fix. Instead, by building empathy, leveraging pivot points, and gradually sharing responsibilities, you can help move your marriage toward a better equilibrium.

Unfortunately, balance is not always possible. If you have a partner with an extremely demanding job, live within a culture where a balanced partnership is not supported, or are raising your family alone, this chapter may feel frustrating. This additional second shift is a burden that you carry every day, and it can negatively impact your work and career prospects.

While there are no easy fixes, seeking out a parent-friendly workplace is a crucial first step. Some companies have extreme time demands and round-the-clock cultures that make it hard to succeed when you don't have support outside of work. Workplace flexibility and a culture of support are doubly important when you lack balance at home.

Beyond the workplace norms, it is also crucial to ensure that you work for a manager who focuses on your output and productivity, not simply hours or face time. During a single year, three women who reported to me announced they were pregnant with their second children. They were anxious about the timing, but having had three kids myself, I was delighted for them. We shuffled their work around and got some backfill support, and they took their full leave. Later, two of them approached me about having to leave at 4:30 p.m. to take the shuttle to make it to childcare pickup. This led to a team conversation about how we did a lot of events at five and were excluding those with children who lived farther away, so we moved the events to start earlier. These were valued and productive employees, and as a manager, I wanted to make sure they were supported and allowed to grow. Not every manager is willing or able to make accommodations, but many are. Finding someone who understands your needs and supports you despite the demands at home can enable you to thrive at work even during the early years of your child's life.

Your Partner as Your Foundation

Many women are inclined to think of their work lives and personal lives as separate, but this is a mistake. These two worlds are tightly linked. A strong partnership at home is the rock on which you build your career. A steady and stable foundation enables you to take risks and make hard choices, while a weak or unsteady one limits you and holds you back.

Abigail Wen couldn't have written her *New York Times* bestseller without a supportive husband, who served as her cheerleader and critique partner as she wrote every night. Andrew encouraged her writing for ten years as they both built successful careers in tech before she signed her first book contract. This gave her the confidence to keep at it even after dozens of rejections until she heard her first "yes."

Rowena Chiu, whom Harvey Weinstein assaulted, was visiting her family outside the country when Jodi Kantor, the *New York Times* investigative reporter and author of *She Said*, paid a surprise visit to her home. Rowena's husband, Andrew Cheung, pushed back against Jodi's request in order to protect his wife who was not ready to share her story. He later went on to help her find an attorney, field questions from journalists, and deal with concerned friends and family.

When she finally decided to go public with her story, Rowena spent six months traveling the world with their toddler so that she could advocate for victims of sexual assault. While working full-time at Facebook, Andrew took care of their three older children, getting them ready for school and putting them to bed each night. He understood the importance of his wife's work and consistently supported her.

Anne-Marie Slaughter's husband, Andrew, enabled her to be one of *Fortune*'s Most Powerful Women because he was the lead parent. Nona Jones's husband is her copastor. Fidji Simo's husband stays home to take care of their daughter so she can run Instacart.

Without David's support and encouragement, I would never have achieved the level of success that I have in my career. I would never have had the time or energy to work full-time while starting a nonprofit, raising three kids, and writing this book.

Behind many powerful women are husbands who provide the stability and support that enable them to thrive. They are full partners at home, encouraging their wives to succeed.

The best career decision I ever made was the choice to date David when I was nineteen and marry him when I was twenty-four. Since then, he has unlocked my potential, pushed me to take risks, and helped me grow my career, all while sharing in every aspect of managing our home and raising our family. Swim lanes enable us to have an equitable household and a peaceable marriage free from resentment.

A strong partnership is the foundation on which you can build your marriage, family, and career. Taking back your power means finding balance at home so that you can thrive at work.

Work and home are yin and yang in your life. In harmony, they can both flourish and blossom, but out of balance, one can throw the other out of whack. Finding that balance will allow you to unlock your full potential.

Find Your Voice

Just like a fingerprint, your voice is unique to you.
—DEB LIU

My Chinese, Christian immigrant parents raised me not to stand out too much. They taught me that hard work would stand on its own and that I shouldn't draw unwanted attention to myself. As immigrants, they focused on carving out a life in a foreign land, hoping to evade too much notice or commentary. As Christians, they stressed the virtues of modesty and humility. I grew up learning these lessons too well, and silencing myself became a way of life. Staying quiet meant staying safe and not risking anything.

I met my husband at Raleigh Chinese Christian Church, where his parents had been founding members and where he had spent many of his formative years. In those times, Chinese churches in southern America embodied a mix of religious, cultural, and social conservatism, modeled after the American churches that helped give rise to them. Having grown up in Southern Baptist and later Presbyterian churches, I was familiar with those norms and expectations. Yet many of the women of the church were leaders, including my future mother-in-law.

Several years later my fiancé and I started the required pre-marital counseling at Atlanta Chinese Christian Church. During one of our sessions, we shared the news that I had been accepted to Stanford Graduate School of Business and that David planned to move with me out to California after we wed. The happy news landed heavily. The pastor of the English-language congregation, who had been counseling us, admonished David harshly. His words stick with me even now, two decades later. "Why are you follow-ing Deborah to California so she can go to graduate school?" he demanded. "You should have the lead career. She should prepare herself to stay home and care for the children."

I didn't know what to say. I was twenty-three, engaged, and dreaming of going to graduate school, and this man was telling me that our joint plans were anathema to the will of God. I sat there stunned, unable to say anything. Embarrassment and shame flooded me. Thoughts ran through my head: "What if he is right? What if I am doing David a disservice? What if this is against God's plan?" I had worked so hard to earn a place at my dream school, and I felt defeated and deflated.

The conservatism of our church and our race stood before me like an immovable object, and I said nothing in the face of that. In our church, a woman's place was the home and hearth, yet the examples of women like my mother and future mother-in-law stood in contrast. They had left their homes and everything they knew to come to America and start anew, and they had worked themselves to the bone to earn degrees. Many women were like them, including many of the women leaders in our church, yet here stood a pastor saying they were all wrong.

My shame turned to anger when David and I later spoke. He reassured me of his commitment to our move and that nothing the pastor said would change that. But I had grown up expecting to be obedient to the church and its teachings. How could I allow myself to go against them?

That's when David said something I will never forget. "Your parents named you Deborah for a reason," he told me. "She was the judge of Israel because God chose her to lead. She preached, prophesied, and led his people. God doesn't make mistakes. And he chose to have a woman lead his people to show the world that it was possible."

He continued, "We read Proverbs 31 together. The Proverbs 31 woman is wife and mother. But she also has her own business, buys her own land, and cares for her family. What does her husband do? He sits at the city gates and hangs out with the guys, no doubt swapping sandals or putting their hands on each other's thighs." I laughed as the ever-erudite David reminded me of how the men of the Old Testament sealed contracts with shoes or by touching one another in agreement.[1]

David encouraged me to reach out to the senior pastor and point out these contradictions. So we sat down with Pastor Jeffrey Lu, the Chinese pastor who led the church, and shared what the English-language pastor had said. He laughed and pointed to his wife, an extremely accomplished woman of faith. Then and there he gave us his blessing and agreed to preside over our ceremony. We married later that year, and one week later, we moved to California to start a new life.

I realized then that my voice mattered, within my relationship and even within the church, a place I considered monolithic and immovable. I had always been taught deference to authority, but I learned an important lesson through this experience. We are given our voices to question the status quo and to seek truth, rather than proceed in blind obedience.

Learning to Speak Up

As I discussed in chapter 2, life is not lived in the margins of safety. It is lived in the moments when you put yourself out there and take a risk, sometimes a scary one. The walls of many conference rooms at Facebook have a poster that reads, "What would you do if you weren't afraid?"

We care about what other people think of us. We worry about how they view our actions, how they judge our choices, and how they measure our successes. We sit in meetings wondering if our comments are insightful enough, ruminating over what other, more influential people say about us.

When I first arrived at Facebook, I joined a team called consumer monetization. The goal was to build a monetization model beyond ads. We spent the next two years developing a strategy for the product that later became the Facebook Credits and Games platform. Because we had a relatively set strategy from the start, most of the executive updates were discussions of our data, approach, and migration plans. We stuck to the clear timeline and delivered milestone after milestone, eventually building an ecosystem worth over $1 billion. This product would account for around 15 percent of the company's revenues when it went public.

When we raised our heads to look around, we realized that no one noticed—or cared.

Though the product was very successful based on objective goals, we had failed at something far more important: the narrative. The team largely disbanded, and most of the members went on to build products across the organization. Still, I never forgot the moment when I realized we had delivered something critical to the future of the company and no one had even noticed.

I went on my last maternity leave dejected, and I debated finding a new role when I returned. At this point the company was about to go public, and I was a little more than two years into the four-year vesting schedule. I knew I had to stick it out for eighteen more months before exploring externally, even though I was incredibly frustrated and unhappy. I was on my seventh manager in two and a half years, and I felt lost within the company and unsure of what was next. When I joined, the company had fewer than a thousand employees. Within a couple of years, it had tripled in size. On the heels of the death of my father and the challenges of a newborn with colic, I only felt more lost. Given the upcoming company initial public offering, and that I had eighteen months of stock left to vest on my initial grant, I wavered as to what to do.

The IPO in May 2012 set the share price at thirty-eight dollars, but it declined to less than half its original value by the fall of that year. I was asked to work on mobile monetization. In those days, "mobile monetization" was code for ads. At first I declined; I had never worked on mobile or ads, and my background was in commerce and payments, which were largely desktop-focused. But I had to wait out my final eighteen months, so I agreed to at least pull together a strategy. That was when I met Vijaye Raji, the first engineer on the product. We spent the rest of the year working on various ideas for mobile monetization, eventually landing on a product called Mobile App Install Ads. At launch, we struggled. Without any data on the market demand for this type of product, we had to instead paint a picture of what the product was not, instead of what it was.

The lesson of Facebook Credits and Games hung like a specter over this new one. Rather than giving facts and metrics, we decided to instead share a narrative. We explained how we were building an app discovery platform that would help developers find their audience. This product went on to generate nearly the same share of the company's revenues, but the reception differed from Credits and Games. Whereas our first product was largely forgotten, the new one went on to become part of company lore. It was the first successful ad vertical at Facebook, and the company went on to build many multibillion-dollar lines of business modeled after it.

The products were not substantially different, but by holding on to the lessons of the first one, I learned to find my voice. I experienced firsthand the power of narrative to shape perception and opportunity.

Learning to Find Your Voice

Sometimes our past teaches us to suppress our voice, to not speak up, or to hide our failures. This protective mechanism works until it reaches its limits and we can no longer live authentically without sharing the full truth.

Carolyn Everson, the former vice president of global marketing solutions at Facebook, had to learn to find her voice—not once but twice. A transformational leader in media and tech for over two decades, she had previously led ad sales at Viacom before going on to run global ad sales and strategy at Microsoft. But she kept a secret from everyone who knew her: she had founded Pets.com, the infamous internet brand of the dot-com boom of the late 1990s. This was something she told nearly no one as she built her career over the next decade.

During her time at Harvard Business School, Carolyn decided to combine her passion for pets and her interest in technology to create a vision for an online service that would help people care for their pets. She found the owner of the Pets.com URL and offered to buy it. In turn, he offered to cofound the company with her. After raising a round of venture capital, Carolyn's lead investor found a CEO to lead the company. Carolyn flew to California to get to know her. After a disastrous meeting that made it clear they didn't agree on the company vision, Carolyn returned to Boston. "By the time I got back to my dorm room, I found out I had been fired (by fax, no less!) from my own company," she recounted.

From there, Carolyn wrote herself out of the story of the company and moved on, leveraging her experience to build a transformative career at multiple media and tech companies. When she started working at Facebook, she realized she didn't want to be only an effective leader; she also wanted to be a leader who exhibited radical openness and authenticity. So she decided to share the story of the most humbling thing that had happened to her.

On stage in front of her entire team, Carolyn reclaimed her experience, recounting how she founded Pets.com only to be fired and how that experience made her a better leader. Her openness inspired her team to lead in a more vulnerable way and share their stories of overcoming past failures.

After sharing her failure, Carolyn believed her journey to finding her voice was complete. Then, one day in June 2021, she left Facebook. Facebook had been her life, and her identity was intertwined with that of the company. She was the face of her team, the voice of the company to a vast set of global clients. For a decade, she had led the Facebook team from revenues of less than $2 billion to $80 billion. She had embraced everything about the company and sacrificed much, traveling more than forty weeks a year to build the business. But she eventually realized she wanted more than the company could offer, and she wanted to break free of the "sales leader" box she had been put in. So she left it all behind.

Carolyn announced her departure and stepped into the unknown. Having worked since she was thirteen, this was the first time she took a leap without having anything lined up. All she knew was that she wanted to find a role where "sales" would not be a modifier to "leader." Leaving a job and a team she loved took courage. Staying felt easy; spreading her wings felt nearly impossible. She had to find her voice again.

By taking her time, Carolyn started to find her footing outside the world she had known for years. This caused her to realize that her voice had for so long not been her own, but rather linked to her role and her company. By rediscovering and reestablishing her identity, she learned that she was so much more than her position and that she was whole without the trappings of a company brand or a big title. Carolyn has committed to writing a book about her experiences as a woman in the male-dominated sales industry and how her brand of authentic leadership can transform both teams and the field at large.

What We Are Taught as Girls

As girls, some of us were taught to silence ourselves. We grow up learning to suppress our opinions or risk being judged. Yet when we look at those who are successful in our society, they are always the bold leaders with strong voices.

Aileen Lee learned these lessons the hard way. As the child of immigrants, she learned to quiet her voice. After graduating from the Massachusetts Institute of Technology, she got a job at Morgan Stanley as a finance analyst. There, she overheard male analysts talking about venture capital, but that seemed out of reach to her at the time. Instead, she headed to Harvard Business School. After graduating in 1997, she took a role at Gap on the team focused on moving the company online. This was during the early days of e-commerce, and she knew little about technology or the industry.

One day Aileen got a call from a recruiter at Kleiner Perkins, a venture capital firm, asking her to interview for a nonpartner track associate position. John Doerr, the Silicon Valley rainmaker, specifically asked the recruiter to seek out women candidates. Aileen hesitated. The company had no women on the investment team at all, and she would be the first at this venerable firm. All eyes would be on her. After deliberating and with the encouragement of female friends, she took the risk and accepted the job.

When Aileen arrived, she noticed something: many men in the industry had formed a tight-knit social circle and had a lot more shared interests. Venture capital felt like an old boys' club, and she was on the outside of it. Aileen was the definition of someone who didn't fit in. She was the youngest, she had not previously worked in a venture-backed startup, she was the only woman, and she was not an engineer. Under the harsh scrutiny of that judgmental culture, Aileen felt little support or room for error. She was rarely invited to socialize; most of the partners were older, married, and likely felt uncomfortable inviting a young woman to events. Partners invited male associates to their houses, flew with them to Vegas, and hung out with them at ballgames and Aileen didn't get the access she later realized was critical to advancement. Whereas partners likely saw something of themselves in her male peers, Aileen and other women who eventually joined the firm, and other firms felt frozen out.

"The attitude of everyone in venture capital at the time was that there were likely a thousand people out there who would kill for our jobs, so women should not complain," she explains. "I didn't want to be seen as high-maintenance, so I stayed silent about any microaggressions, harassment, and different treatment. For women to survive in our roles, we had the tacit understanding that if we made [the partners] uncomfortable, they would want to work with us less, and we would get even less access."

As I mentioned earlier, venture capital as an industry has always been dominated by men. Today less than 10 percent of investors in venture are women, and an even smaller share of funds are founded by and led by women.[2]

For years Aileen tried to get along by staying quiet. She knew that in life men were given the benefit of the doubt, and women, especially minority women, were not. As a junior associate, she observed founders come in and pitch. She took copious notes, writing down her observations in detail. She realized that her insights and instincts were being proven correct. Slowly, she learned to speak up—tentatively at first, and more firmly as time went on. "I took the slow boat to finding my voice," she recalls.

In 2012 her colleague and friend Ellen Pao, who had joined in 2005, was passed over for a senior partner position despite being promised it by John Doerr. During this same period, several men were promoted past her. That year, Ellen sued Kleiner Perkins for gender discrimination.[3] "Ellen was very brave," Aileen reflects. "Women who step up and raise their hands to complain about inequity are fighting an uphill battle against big companies with big law firms and deep pockets. Even though she didn't win, what happened became public record, and it was in many ways a landmark case for our industry."

That same year, Aileen started her own venture fund, Cowboy Ventures, and there she truly came into her voice. For years she had held back, with both tacit and explicit signals reminding her of her place. Now, without the constraints of a large firm, she was able to speak out about gender and racial disparities in the industry and the positions women were being placed in. She drew attention to these challenges, including how informal networks create uneven playing fields for women, both as investors and as founders. "I got a chance to restart without the legacy power dynamics," she explains. "I found my voice and learned to speak up."

At the height of the #MeToo movement in 2017, Aileen sent out an email to the women investors in her network to connect about what they could do to change their industry.[4] Within a few months, she had gathered thirty-four women venture leaders committed to bringing more women into the field and encouraging investment in more women founders. This was how All Raise, a nonprofit cofounded by many of the most senior women in venture capital, was born.[5] The group realized that a unified voice from women across their industry could amplify the message more than one person could alone.

Whenever anyone talks about Aileen, one of the first things they cite is that she coined the industry term *unicorn*, referring to billion-dollar startups, in an article for TechCrunch, a tech insider news site.[6] The second thing they note is her refreshing outspokenness and candor. The things women know and feel, but only say in private, Aileen is willing to say out loud. Much of her message resonates, but some friends and colleagues have encouraged her to temper it. "I've been told, 'It could blow up in your face,' or, 'Be careful,'" Aileen says. "But we can't continue to pretend that bias is not rampant in our industry, or other industries. I am tired of people saying, 'Oh, he is a good guy' when discussing a man for a role, then questioning the specific skills of an equally qualified woman. Men continue to get better financial terms and raise more money than women. I have the privilege to call out things that we all see. It can be a little scary, so I'm grateful to have the support of folks who say it is helping to make a positive difference."

Aileen went from silence to finding her voice and speaking out on behalf of those who don't have the clout and influence she has. But her fight is not done. She is joining together with hundreds of VCs and founders to change the way the industry treats women and minority investors and founders, thus helping others find their own voices.

Speaking Up and Standing Out

There is cognitive dissonance in the workplace. Our culture rewards those who stand out, speak up, or make their voices heard. We want our leaders to be bold, outspoken, and charismatic, but we grow up following the definitions of what a woman "should" be.

My daughter Danielle's teacher said during a parent-teacher conference, "Math has become a boys' club. The girls don't raise their hands, and they don't speak up." When we asked her about it, Danielle shrugged and replied, "The boys are just better at it." They are ten years old. Girls are getting signals early on that boys do math and girls should not take up space. Try as we might, we are fighting acculturation that starts young.

The challenge of speaking up has created a dangerous double bind. When women speak up, they are interrupted 33 percent more by their male colleagues than they would be if they were men.[7] Their voices are often drowned out, silenced, or ignored. Even powerful women, like those on the Supreme Court, are not immune and are interrupted significantly more than their male counterparts. Given this silencing, it is easy to choose to sit out or step back.

I struggled with speaking up for so long. As a natural introvert, I spoke only when I knew I had the right answer, rarely daring to speculate or debate. Most women learn to stifle their voices because we train them to. I remember attending a dinner of senior executives, primarily male, when someone asked a question about commerce at Facebook, my area of expertise. I started to speak, only for a male peer who worked in a different area to speak over me. For nearly ten minutes, I listened to him talk about a space I had built multiple products in for over fifteen years, and I said nothing, unable to respond or react. I knew that talking over him wasn't an option, and I grappled with what to do. I didn't want to appear abrasive or overly forceful because I knew I would be judged harshly. I gave away my power because I didn't have the courage to speak up.

Women learn in the workplace that having a voice has its costs, and this has been proven over and over, both in experimental studies and in real life.[8] Women perceived to be "assertive" are judged to be substantially less competent, even though assertiveness is a quality we associate with leadership.[9] Female CEOs who speak more and in more powerful ways are viewed negatively as leaders and seen as less qualified for the role—by both men and women.[10] In one study, when mixed-gender groups of five were given an assignment, women spoke only two-thirds as much as men.[11] Gradually, we have taught women to stifle their voices to avoid drawing comments or appearing disagreeable, especially when underrepresented in the group.

This can feel like an unwinnable situation. Talk too much or appear too forceful, and you are considered less competent. Don't speak enough, and you are perceived as lacking influence. We are forced to walk a tightrope, constantly balancing between two chasms and having to overthink every word.

And sometimes we are erased from the story altogether.

The legend of the PayPal Mafia has been told and retold over the past two decades. The founders and early employees of PayPal were photographed together dressed up as gangsters for *Fortune* magazine in 2007.[12] This well-known group included legendary investors, founders, and visionaries, including Peter Thiel (cofounder of PayPal, Palantir), Elon Musk (founder of SpaceX), Max Levchin (cofounder of PayPal, Affirm), David Sacks (cofounder of Yammer), Roelof Botha (Sequoia partner), Steve Chen (cofounder of YouTube), Reid Hoffman (cofounder of LinkedIn), Jeremy Stoppelman (cofounder of Yelp), and more. But not a single woman was invited to be in this photograph, including the one woman who worked hand in hand with these men to build PayPal to what it became: Amy Klement.

Amy joined X.com, the precursor to PayPal, early in 1999. After the merger, she was the vice president of product at PayPal. For years the legend of the PayPal Mafia grew, and Amy watched as her colleagues, including some she had hired and mentored, went on to be heralded while she and her female colleagues were left out of the story. She rarely spoke about her role in the early creation of PayPal or her role as the head of product and design, which she led long after many of the original members of PayPal's early team left.

With a deep passion for people, Amy mentored and fostered many successful product and design leaders in the industry during her tenure. Many went on to become CEOs, founders, C-suite executives, investors, and board members throughout Silicon Valley. Her legacy has been felt throughout the industry, but her name doesn't appear beside the pantheon of men she worked beside.

"Women are often written out of the stories of successful companies. We are pushed to the background or forgotten," Amy wrote. "But I chose to look forward rather than to look back. As I followed my passion into my next chapter, I committed to ensure the story was truly representative and inclusive . . . The questions I challenge all women to ask themselves are, 'What story are you creating?' and, 'Who are you writing into your story?'"

For Amy, that next chapter was outside the heart of tech in Silicon Valley. She stepped down from her role as an executive at eBay (at the time, parent company to PayPal) to become a partner at Omidyar Network, where she invested in mission-driven entrepreneurs in emerging markets. For the past decade, she has led investments in health, financial inclusion, energy, and consumer tech, with a growing concentration on education. Last year she founded and became CEO of Imaginable Futures, a philanthropic investment firm backed by Pierre and Pam Omidyar. With over $240 million invested, the firm's mission is to unlock human potential through learning.

Amy found her voice by looking forward and not back. Rather than allowing herself to be erased from the narrative, she chose to rewrite her story by looking to the future and elevating those who have no voice.

If you ask someone to envision a leader, a CEO, what do they think of? A bold visionary. A loud, imposing voice. A man.

Certainly not me, an introverted Asian American woman. I learned the danger of overstepping my bounds early on, constantly being told in reviews that I was "difficult," "pushy," "too aggressive," or "hard to get along with." I saw men who talked over me repeatedly get praised, while the women around me were judged viciously for minor missteps.

A woman mentor told me early in my career, "The key to a woman's success in Silicon Valley is learning to work with difficult men."

That struck me as unfair. I pushed back and asked, "When do *they* have to learn to work with *us*?"

She laughed and replied, "Never." She told me to open my eyes and look around. "This is their world."

Those words stuck with me through every performance review telling me I pushed too hard for my product or that I spoke up too much despite speaking less than others. I learned to stifle my voice and use my words carefully so as not to offend. I debated what to say every time I opened my mouth, trying to balance expertise and influence.

During my early years at Facebook, I struggled to find my footing. I had gone from the director of the buyer experience at eBay to the equivalent of a senior product manager at Facebook, essentially pushing back my career by nearly a decade. I cycled through seven managers in two and a half years, and each promised a promotion only if I hit the next milestone. Despite all my hard work and product successes, I still couldn't get promoted.

I mentioned that learning to open up while I was at Facebook was a difficult process. This was a company focused on bringing the world closer together, and it was common practice to connect with your colleagues on the site itself as you met them in real life. While I found this daunting, it became the ultimate test. For me, the hardest part was worrying that I had nothing to say that was worth listening to. Having a voice meant being vulnerable, something I was reluctant to do.

Over time, I found that sharing more of myself wasn't a weakness but an opportunity to connect. So I gradually came out of my comfort zone. I started posting anecdotes about my children, tagging each of the posts #mommyschool, a term that my then-two-year-old son coined. At first I felt self-conscious, until people started talking about how the posts touched them or made them laugh. It broke the ice and opened the door for more communication.

As you grow into your own voice, please know that the sentiment you leave is more important than the mere words you say. If you are open, even when it's difficult, others will be open with you too. Your voice is a way to create a connection that didn't exist before.

Maintain Your Voice

The hard part about putting yourself out there is that sometimes it won't work. People will call you out or say you are too vocal, that you are being too forward or saying too much. There is a price to pay for every expectation you break and every stereotype you defy.

But there is a greater price for *not* questioning the rules and breaking free of preconceptions. Conforming can be easier and safer, but it also makes it harder to be perceived as a leader. Think back to your idea of what a leader looks like. When you close your eyes and imagine, does that leader look like you?

Just like a fingerprint, your voice is unique to you. It is your story, perspective, and passion. Part of this journey is finding that authentic part of yourself and putting it out there. Whatever it looks like to you, find a way to make it real to others. Sharing opens the door to connection, vulnerability, and, ultimately, trust. Silence is the enemy of authentic leadership, and your voice is the key to breaking through.

Make Your Mark

I don't want to spend my life waiting to die. I choose
to live fully for as long as I have.
—STACY GENERAL

During a class in graduate school, my classmates and I were once asked to write our obituaries and submit them as an assignment. Many of us laughed. We were a group of ambitious twenty-somethings with little idea of what the world held in store for us. After reading through what we had written, our professor summarized the last chapters of our stories for us. He talked about our accomplishments, our families, and our regrets. Some of my classmates foresaw themselves founding companies, while others planned to become CEOs. Still others talked about being influential writers or leaders. The two things our professor said our stories had in common were that we all lived to an advanced age, many well into our nineties, and that all of us were outlived by our spouses (save one, who predicted passing away immediately after his wife).

"Apparently none of you want to deal with grief and would rather others grieve you," our professor quipped. We all had a good laugh, not knowing what was to come.

That exercise became more salient when we returned for our fifteen-year class reunion in 2017. During the intervening years, we had lost two members of our graduating class. As I stood with over a hundred of my classmates, listening to a tribute to the lives of those who were gone, I thought back to that day in class. None of us who laughed then could have imagined that two of those obituaries would be published so soon.

Often as we live our day-to-day lives, it is hard to imagine the end of our story and consider what we will leave behind. But that exercise in business school helped me focus on what I wanted to prioritize in my life and how I wanted my story to turn out. Few people in that class wrote about having a lot of money or possessions. Instead, most shared their hopes for their family and the positive impact they wanted to have on the world.

Taking back your power means taking control of the end of your story and then working backward from then to now. Where do you ultimately want to be, and what do you hope to have accomplished? Writing your ending may seem macabre or depressing, but it is actually an act of hope. If you hope for a life well-lived, knowing what that looks like means you can actively strive for it every single day.

There are three components to making your mark.

1. Draft your obituary.
2. Craft your vision.
3. Create annual milestones.

Draft Your Obituary: Write the Last Chapter First

When companies prepare products for launch, the team does an exercise called a "premortem." During a premortem, everyone on the team sits together in a room and writes out the worst things that could happen when a product goes out. This adversarial strategy helps teams foresee potential pitfalls, plan to prevent them, and build contingency plans in case of failure.

Many organizations do postmortems after things have gone wrong. After the *Columbia* shuttle loss, NASA put out a multivolume report going through, in detail, every technical issue, decision, and cultural challenge that led to the tragedy.[1] When the Republicans lost the presidential race in 2012, they surveyed or spoke to more than fifty thousand people, publishing a new road map for the party, popularly known as "The Autopsy."[2] When the Democrats lost the 2016 election, multiple parties wrote postmortems, assessing everything from Hillary Clinton's ground game to last-minute voters breaking for Donald Trump after FBI Director James Comey's press conference. In each of these cases, assessing the flaws after the fact gave a clear picture of which events led to the failure and which approaches could be used to avoid the same outcome in the future.

Looking back on mistakes is useful. It means you can adjust your course to avoid making them again. But at the end of life, there is no postmortem, no second chance to do it right next time. The flow of time means the ending is truly the end, not a chance to look back on what you can do differently. Instead, you can take initiative by writing your last chapter first.

Imagine you are sitting down to write your obituary. What do you want it to say? How do you want to be remembered? What you write will illustrate the values you hold most dear. These will be your guide as you live your life, your north star as you go on your journey.

Take one evening to write your obituary, and then set it aside. Read it again a week later, and then a month later, and then refine it. After that, tuck it away and review it once a year. It will be your road map for where and how you invest your energy.

Writing the story of your life from the end may seem like a futile exercise. The idea of dwelling on a moment that is potentially decades away feels like a waste of time when you probably still have a lot of life left to live. But the passage of time becomes more salient when every day feels finite and measurable. Stacy General knows this well.

In 2005, four months after her wedding to her new husband, Victor General III, Stacy Lee General received the devastating news that she had metastatic mucinous adenocarcinoma of the appendix, a rare cancer that occurs in only one in a million people.[3] She was thirty-one. After three years of treating her, her surgeon gave up and said there was nothing further he could do. Stacy found herself facing down her remaining time with stage IV cancer, knowing the five-year survival rate for her disease was below 20 percent.[4]

Ever the problem solver, Stacy sought another way. This tenacity led her to a specialist who has been pushing the boundaries of what's possible. Together, they have kept her cancer in check for the past fifteen years.

Stacy was a born fighter. Growing up with a largely absent father and a poor mother who suffered from mental illness, she knew from a young age that she wanted more and would push herself to get it. Knowing she would have to pay her own way through school, she worked two jobs to put herself through San Jose State University. She then secured an internship at Ann Taylor, where she worked for five years, before joining eBay in 1999, when it was still in its early stages of growth.

Stacy suddenly found herself in the heart of Silicon Valley, surrounded by people, especially men, from prestigious universities. Because she was a mixed-race woman from a state school, her imposter syndrome made her question whether she had the same qualifications and abilities as the Stanford and Harvard graduates around her.

Later, Stacy transferred to eBay's newly acquired payments company, PayPal, which at the time had only several hundred employees, to lead consumer marketing. She grew her career even as her cancer spread, taking on new challenges and building a team to tackle emerging businesses and ventures on PayPal's behalf.

Despite her personal challenges, Stacy knew she couldn't let cancer define her, so she took a chance on a new role at Facebook, which had a reputation for its intense culture. Stacy remained undaunted. "I am not lesser because I have cancer," she said. "I'm confident in myself and my capabilities. I lead from a place of genuine care. I have a unique perspective that enables me to tackle hard, messy, seemingly insurmountable challenges . . . because I've been through worse."

As Facebook scaled its consumer marketing efforts, the senior leadership of the marketing organization called on Stacy to lead the branding campaign for the Facebook app. This was a challenge given the negative industry sentiment at the time. Stacy launched the "More Together" ad campaign, which included the company's first Super Bowl TV commercial, in 2020, highlighting Facebook as a place for community and connection.

Over the course of her career and successes, Stacy knew she had to balance her work with her health challenges. Appendix cancer manifests as a result of cancer cells spreading widely throughout the abdomen and attaching to various organs. Since her diagnosis, Stacy has undergone a major tumor debulking surgery—often referred to as the "mother of all surgeries" by those who have undergone it—eight times.[5] Each surgery required months of recovery, and through the years she has had more than half a dozen of her organs removed, either in part or in full. These surgeries have taken their toll, and she now walks with a brace and walker. Meanwhile, she has also undergone multiple difficult chemotherapy treatments and continues to undergo surgeries every six weeks simply to maintain her kidney function.

Stacy has never let cancer define her. She adopted a son from Ethiopia over a decade ago, and every day, she shows her love for him, fighting for every opportunity to remain with him for as long as they have together. She knows the end of her story could come any time, so she's decided to make the most of her journey, both the good and the bad. She has beaten the odds over and over, pushing herself to live life to the fullest. Stacy knows how she wants her story to end, and she plans to go out fighting.

Craft Your Vision: Your Legacy as Your North Star

When I took the CEO role at Ancestry, I went in not knowing what to expect. I interviewed for the role via Zoom and never met any of the board or leadership team in person. Because of the confidential nature of who was being hired for the role, the first time I met my new executive team was via a blind video conference. Each of the executives on the senior leadership team was given a Zoom link and meeting time without knowing who would show up on the other side as their new CEO.

The first thing I did when I arrived at Ancestry was a listening tour. For the first thirty days, I spoke to more than seventy people throughout the company. I listened to their hopes and concerns regarding the new leadership and what it meant for them. By the end of the month, I had crafted a new vision statement that encapsulated what I heard. This vision statement became the north star of my tenure at the company and served as the guide for everything we did. From that vision, we updated our priorities and goals, eventually leading to changes in execution and accountability throughout the organization.

Similarly, a personal vision statement is like a road map. It represents what you want your legacy to be. This statement should encompass your purpose and why you choose to do what you do. Mine is a simple reminder that I wrote to guide my actions:

> God gave us a short time to make our mark, so I want to live each day with purpose. I want to leave people better for having met me. I am a problem solver, connector, and creator, so I will use these skills to live with no regrets.

I wrote this vision to help guide me in the choices I made, both things I said yes to and those I said no to. This vision has led me to where I am today. It inspired me to mentor over a thousand strangers, coaching them through their career challenges. It drove me to write each night, publishing weekly articles and eventually writing this book. It helped me to get over my fear of the unknown and taught me to live my life looking forward, not backward.

Vision statements can help shape your life's work, and they can come unexpectedly. CC Lee's purpose catalyzed in a single moment, a chance encounter that set her life on a new path.

Growing up the child of immigrants in Columbia, South Carolina, CC always dreamed of pursuing science. After winning a full scholarship to Duke University, she took on the notoriously difficult biomedical engineering major and graduated with honors. She went on to earn her medical degree from Harvard Medical School.

In 2004, upon completing her residency in pediatrics, CC and her new husband, Marty, started volunteering at a clinic in Yushu, Qinghai, that had no running water or electricity. They did this for months at a time for four years.

Yushu is a remote Tibetan prefecture located high in the Himalayas, inhabited largely by nomads who earn less than a dollar a day. While Marty used his civil engineering training to try to bring water to the facility, CC started seeing patients, teaching local health workers how to support mothers and their newborns, and delivering babies in local nomadic tents. One day she watched a mother lose her baby to asphyxia, suffocation caused by a botched birth. CC knew in her heart that she could have saved that baby if only she had arrived at the tent earlier to resuscitate the baby in its precious first minutes of life. "I knew I wanted to dedicate the rest of my life to saving the mothers and babies like the one I couldn't save that day," she said. This tragedy propelled her to devote her life to maternal and infant care in places where basic medical care is largely unavailable.

CC spent the next fifteen years traveling the world every couple of months, going to remote villages and rural areas to understand the challenges of maternal and infant mortality. She has helped create programs to train local health workers to reduce infectious diseases from tainted water and studied how to prevent maternal transmission of infections to babies during birthing. She also extensively studied how to prevent birth asphyxia, the seminal tragedy that had set her on her path. She currently leads the Global Advancement of Infants and Mothers Lab at the Brigham and Women's Hospital.

A mother of four herself, CC knows how fragile life can be for newborns. When her first child, Liam, was born in 2008, he developed severe jaundice. She returned to the hospital on Liam's third day of life, when his bilirubin had risen to a dangerous level. He spent a week in the hospital getting phototherapy treatment.

CC witnessed firsthand the effect that this condition can have on vulnerable newborns when left untreated. Undiagnosed jaundice in infants may cause irreversible brain damage, and in severe cases, death. Most American hospitals are equipped with laboratories for blood testing or noninvasive devices costing upward of $7,000 to screen babies for jaundice, and thus permanent impairment from it in the United States is rare. But in many countries like India, Eswatini, and Bangladesh, where CC traveled to research and practice medicine, screening is not common and testing is often not available. Access to treatment is also extremely limited. CC tended to the needs of multiple babies affected by jaundice every day. Much of the damage was preventable and treatable. Over a million children per year suffer from severe jaundice, including my own son, and CC knew that without a change in the screening and testing process, many of these children in the poorest countries would continue to suffer.

After her son's birth, CC pondered the complex problem of diagnosing jaundice. After years of testing and research, she developed the bili-ruler: a simple printed plastic ruler that, when pressed against a newborn's skin, determines their level of bilirubin.[6] This allows anyone to test babies for jaundice. CC has been able to prove through research that this piece of plastic, which costs only a few dollars to manufacture, can accurately detect jaundice in field studies in different settings. Her work has the potential to help identify high-risk newborns suffering from this preventable condition. Preliminary estimates show that her invention could touch one million babies by 2030. CC made her mark on the world by finding her purpose and then pursuing it with passion. She quipped, "I have no regrets and have never taken the easy path. I drive a duct-taped minivan and a thirteen-year-old Prius . . . we live in a very old farmhouse far outside of Boston. Yet I have four healthy children with opportunities that many children across the world do not have. This inspires me every day to serve the mothers and babies across the world who do not have the basic access to high-quality health care that we have had." CC's legacy will live on far beyond her research, her title, and her grant awards.

Create Annual Milestones: Using Markers to Progress

Once you know how you want your story to end and what you want your legacy to be, the next step is to make progress toward making your mark. That means being willing to change your life by setting clear goals and milestones.

The human mind has a hard time grasping the concept of time. Children often talk about how slowly time seems to pass as they await growing up, but for adults, time seems to fly by in a flurry of responsibility and obligation. Taking a step back to create milestones and mark time can help you work toward your legacy in a measurable way.

Breaking down a problem makes it achievable. Rather than getting caught up in the day-to-day, you can use setting and noting your progress as a way to move forward. For CC, that meant planning multiple trips to areas of greatest need and publishing groundbreaking research each year. For Abigail Wen, it meant completing a manuscript every two years, even when it took her more than a decade to get the first one published. For me, it means setting statements of purpose through New Year's resolutions every January 1. For the past nineteen years, I have leveraged this annual moment to evolve my life in the direction I want it to go.

Start with your legacy and work backward to today, this moment. Break down what you hope to leave behind, and start marking your progress from now. What will you do within the next 365 days to take you closer to what you want to leave behind? Which building blocks do you need to achieve what you aspire to? How will you approach each day to ensure you live your life with purpose?

Since 2015, I've posted my annual resolutions on Facebook. Every January 1, I evaluate how I've done on the past year's goals and set goals for the following year. This allows me to reflect on what progress I have been able to make and what I hope to change. What's been fascinating in rereading these reflections is how much I have changed my life, one annual statement at a time.

Carolyn Everson, whose story I told in the previous chapter, used this practice to transform her life and her work. She genuinely believed in a radical transparency that other leaders only paid lip service to, so she began posting her biannual performance review to her whole team. She opened up about her family, including her father's fragile health and ultimate passing and her mother's mental state as she watched him decline. Carolyn took vulnerability to a new level. People on her team didn't want a leader who was perfect or untouchable. They wanted someone authentic who understood failure and hardship but also aspired to more.

Her desire to be transparent eventually led Carolyn to write an annual statement, after getting the idea from Lisa McCarthy, founder of the leadership consultancy group Fast Forward. Carolyn has not only written one for herself each year, starting in 2013, but she also asks her four-thousand-person team to do so as well. This has helped her craft her path intentionally and with purpose and to never take anything for granted.

"I [write] an annual vision statement: essentially, a letter to myself dated one year in the future, outlining all of the things I have accomplished in that year," she explains. "I write—in acute detail— what I have enacted across the three elements of my life: my personal initiatives, professional goals, and community service work."[7]

That vision statement turned into Carolyn's guide for each year, forcing her to reflect on what she plans to accomplish before even starting it. This gives her purpose and meaning and has propelled her to become one of the most effective sales leaders in the world. Each of these statements is precious to her. They remind her of who she aspired to be each year and have made her who she is today.

Your Mark Is Your Legacy

This book is about taking back your power in the workplace, but in the end, you are far more than your job and your career. You are more than a title, a LinkedIn profile, or the size of your team. You are a combination of all your successes and challenges, and you are the narrative of a life lived as our world rapidly changes. No matter where you are in your life, it is never too late to recapture and pursue your legacy.

In 2007, at age fifty-seven, Arianna Huffington was working nonstop to build her new venture, *The Huffington Post*, an online news site she had launched two years before. Once, after working through the night, she collapsed, waking up in a pool of blood with a broken cheekbone. "It was a true wake-up call," she recounts. After being diagnosed with burnout, she sought to understand the relationship between well-being and work productivity. "What I found out," she explains, "was not that I had been successful because I'd burned myself out, but in spite of it."

In 2011, AOL bought *The Huffington Post* for $315 million and named Arianna the head of The Huffington Post Media Group, which included their other media properties, such as AOL Content and Music, TechCrunch, Engadget, and Patch.[8] While leading this media empire, she took inspiration from her burnout and wrote two bestselling books, *Thrive* and *The Sleep Revolution*. She realized she wanted to make her mark by helping others thrive, so she left AOL to found Thrive Global at age sixty-six.

Arianna reminded me repeatedly to share the age at which she founded her companies. She wanted to emphasize that it is never too late to build your legacy. Women are often judged harshly as they age, but Arianna saw that she could take all her wisdom and experience and become an entrepreneur at an age when others usually consider retiring. Her story is a reminder that your path is not set and that it is never too late to start pursuing your dreams.

As you consider how to make your mark, think about what each day means to you.

When two people encounter each other, they have the power to change each other's paths. Over the past eight years, I have had an open-door policy where I will meet with anyone who asks—first at Facebook, and then openly within the industry. Over the years, I have met with more than a thousand people. Most came with a specific question, like which path to choose, and many sought career advice. Some were in difficult circumstances or wanted help handling a challenging situation with a manager or a peer. Others aspired to more but didn't know how to get there.

When I decided to change roles in 2021, more than a hundred people reached out and shared how meeting me changed their paths in some small way. Many people reminded me of something I had said during one of these brief meetings, something that helped them at a time when they needed support or advice. Several even quoted my words back to me and shared the impact that they had. The humbling thing was that I couldn't remember most of what I had said, but they remembered.

That was when I realized how profoundly we affect one another through our words and deeds, without even knowing it. When you consider how you want to make your mark, consider not the accolades and awards, the titles and promotions, but how you live your life and how you impact those around you. Your mark is your legacy, what others will say during your eulogy. Your mark is those you leave behind, who will carry on your mission and pay it forward. Your mark is your voice as it echoes through the lives of those you meet during the short time you have here on earth. Decide what that mark is to you, and pursue it with a passion.

Looking to the Future

As a child growing up in a small town, I internalized the negative messages that being different meant being "the other" and that I should go back to where I came from. Bewildered and alienated, I spent years feeling angry that my parents made us leave our old lives behind to go to a place where I was never accepted or even tolerated. I let this anger become the rocket fuel that drove my desire to succeed, to show the world that I was worthy of acceptance.

The hydrogen in rocket fuel is so powerful that it can propel humans into space, but it is also so highly combustible that, if misused, it can destroy everything around it. One day Sheryl Sandberg pulled me aside after a product review with the executive team and said, "You can stop fighting now. You've won." She saw the chip on my shoulder and called me out on it. That was when I realized that my anger had gotten me to where I was but that it had stopped being useful long ago. I had reached the point where the power that my resentment had given me during my childhood threatened to destroy everything that I wanted to achieve.

From that moment, I decided to stop fighting and proving and instead start connecting and building. It was a hard pivot for me, having achieved so much from that well of negative emotions, to learn to find the grace to fuel my next chapter. Once I realized I had nothing left to prove, I began to realize I had unwittingly given my power to those who had once hurt me. Now was my chance to take it back.

Our time in this world is limited, and we can't always control our circumstances. But we can always choose to learn and benefit from our experiences and leave behind a legacy that aligns with who we want to be. Your own experience can hold you back or be a guiding light. You get to choose every day whether to let your past define you or be the stepping-stone to your future.

Don't allow life to define you. Seek to define your life. This is the ultimate way you can take back your power.

Afterword

Life is 10% about what happens to me and 90% how
I react to it.

—CHUCK SWINDOLL

When I set out to write this book, I knew there was no secret to success—no magical step-by-step, one-size-fits-all plan for making it as a woman in the workplace. Success is equal parts luck, motivation, and execution. Life gives us different opportunities, challenges, and raw talents. This book is a guide to taking what we have been given and making the most of it. We can allow our experiences and setbacks be hindrances, or we can turn them into fuel to take us further than we ever expected.

Life is not fair. The playing field is not level. The second shift exists. The expectations between men and women are unequal. You will be interrupted. You will be passed over. You will be turned down.

I wish I could have written a book about how we could fix the system together. If I had a magic wand, that's what I would want for all of us. That was what Lenore and her friends at Berkeley aspired to over forty years ago, when they fought to level the playing field by bringing more girls into STEM. Today, in their seventies, they are still fighting for women to take an equal place alongside their male peers.

But this book is not about how hopelessly unfair the workplace is. On the contrary, this is a book about hope. I write these words in the hope of showing you that in every challenge, there is an opportunity. The trail you walk may be rockier than those of others, but it is yours to blaze. Your journey may present obstacles and stumbling blocks, but you have the strength to overcome them.

You don't get to decide what happens to you in your life, but you get to decide what you do in response. As you close these pages, I hope you remember that while you can't change everything, you have more power than you think. You can and should affect the events around you. You have allies. You have opportunities. You have a voice that is unique to you, a story to share, and a difference to make in the world.

I hope that one day my daughters, who are ten and thirteen as I put down this pen, will read these words. I hope on that day they will laugh at how anachronistic my advice is. I hope they will think back to when these words were written as they grow their careers and joke with each other about how crazy things were back then. Until that day comes, they have a journey to take and lives to shape—and so do you.

Craft a path that is uniquely yours. Create the world you want to see. Take back your power.

Acknowledgments

The atomic unit of success is not an individual; it is a team. This is also true of writing a book. I could not have completed this book without the many people who have encouraged, supported, and helped me every step of the way.

First and foremost, I am grateful and blessed to be married to David Liu, the most patient and understanding husband in the world. Little did I know when we met over two decades ago what adventures we would have together. And to my three not-always-so-patient kids, Danielle, Bethany, and Jonathan, thank you for letting me tell our story. Bethany, I promise that in a future book I will do the dedication in alphabetical order so the middle child can be first for once. Way to take back your power by asking for what you want!

To my parents, who came to the United States to live the American dream, I hope that our family legacy is worth the sacrifice you made to make our lives here a success. I am only sorry that Dad didn't live to see our story in print, but I am glad Mom has survived multiple bouts of cancer to perhaps hold this book in her hands. To my sister, Caroline Lau, who put up with all those angsty years, I thank you for always encouraging me while also telling me the truth and reminding me that no matter what I accomplish, I will always be your little sister.

Thank you to my New Leaf Literary agents, Kathleen Ortiz and Stephanie Kim, who stuck with me through a multiyear journey to complete this project. They took a risk on an unknown author and helped a writing newbie turn an idea into what has now become this book.

Special thanks to the Zondervan team: Carolyn McCready, Webster Younce, Kim Tanner, Paul Fisher, Alicia Kasen, Devin Duke, and Matt Bray. You have shown me what is possible when someone believes in you. I knew from our first meeting that Zondervan would be the right home for this book and everything that is to come.

To my sponsors and mentors who built my career, I would not be here without you. I have had many, and I wish I could include you all here. Amy Klement, you took a chance on me, even when I hadn't earned it. Doug Purdy, you taught me to believe in the power of possibility. Mike Vernal, you were my ally and counsel. Andrew Bosworth, you taught me to open up and encouraged me to write, even when I was sure I had nothing to say. Sheryl Sandberg, you saw my potential, and your plainspoken feedback pushed me to be more than I thought I could be.

I would also like to thank the incredible women who made this book possible: The ladies of our church small group, Yvonne Chou, Mary Ann Kim, Kelly Lu, and Miki Wetzler, who patiently listened and supported me through this endeavor. Zainab Ghadiyali, who not only gave me the idea to write this book but also introduced me to the New Leaf team. Lisa Revelli, who pushed through many barriers to enable me to complete this project. Isabella Bailey, who supported me through the whole writing process, even when it felt like it wasn't going to come together. Abigail Wen, who showed me it was possible to achieve our dreams as writers even if it felt so far away.

To the coaches and cheerleaders in my life, Katia Verresen, Sanyin Siang, Carol Isozaki, and Scott Cook, thank you for pushing me to do what you all believed I was capable of.

To Professor Jeffrey Pfeffer, at whose Stanford Graduate School of Business class Paths to Power I have spoken for the past seven years: without your encouragement and inspiration, I would never have written this book.

Lastly, to each of the amazing women I interviewed, thank you for allowing me to tell your stories and to share your hard-won wisdom with the world. I hope others will learn as much from each of you as I have.

Notes

Why You Need This Book

1. Lexico, s.v. "power," accessed November 22, 2021, https://www. lexico.com/en/definition/power.

2. Lisa Richards, "Women in Engineering at Duke University," (research paper, Duke University, 2006), 38, https://dukespace .lib.duke.edu/dspace/bitstream/handle/10161/221/Richards _L-Women%20in%20EGR-1.pdf?sequence=1&isAllowed=y.

3. "About Duke Engineering," Pratt School of Engineering, Duke University, updated December 21, 2021, https://pratt.duke.edu /about; "Employed Persons by Detailed Occupation, Sex, Race, and Hispanic or Latino Ethnicity," Current Population Survey, U. S. Bureau of Labor Statistics, accessed December 1, 2021, https://www.bls.gov/cps/cpsaat11.htm.

4. Susan S. Silbey, "Why Do So Many Women Who Study Engineering Leave the Field?" *Harvard Business Review*, August 23, 2016, https:// hbr.org/2016/08/why-do-so-many-women-who-study-engineering -leave-the-field.

5. Alisha Haridasani Gupta, "California Companies Are Rushing to Find Female Board Members," *New York Times*, updated January 14, 2020, https://www.nytimes.com/2019/12/17/us/california -boardroom-gender-quota.html.

6. Jess Huang et al., "Women in the Workplace 2019," *McKinsey & Company*, accessed January 20, 2022, https://www.mckinsey.com /featured-insights/diversity-and-inclusion/women-in-the-workplace. See: But a "broken rung" prevents women from reaching the top.

7. Anne Dennon, "As College Gender Gap Widens, Gender Pay

Gap Slowly Shrinks," BestColleges, September 27, 2021, https://
bestcolleges.com/news/analysis/2021/09/27/college-gender-gap
-widens-gender-pay-gap-shrinks/.

Rule #1: Know Your Playing Field

1. Lexico, s.v. "power," accessed November 22, 2021, https://www.lexico
   .com/en/definition/power.
2. "The Simple Truth about the Gender Pay Gap: 2021 Update,"
   AAUW, 1–6, accessed January 20, 2022, https://www.aauw.org/app
   /uploads/2021/09/AAUW_SimpleTruth_2021_-fall_update.pdf.
3. Benjamin Artz, Amanda Goodall, and Andrew J. Oswald, "Research:
   Women Ask for Raises as Often as Men, but Are Less Likely to Get
   Them," *Harvard Business Review*, June 25, 2018, https://hbr.org/2018
   /06/research-women-ask-for-raises-as-often-as-men-but-are-less
   -likely-to-get-them.
4. Minda Zetlin, "Want to Raise Successful Daughters? Be Careful Not
   to Do This," *Inc.*, August 30, 2018, https://www.inc.com/minda
   -zetlin/daughters-chores-allowance-gender-bias-sexism-fairness
   -parenting.html.
5. Soraya Chemaly, "All Teachers Should Be Trained to Overcome Their
   Hidden Biases," *Time*, February 12, 2015, https://time.com/3705454
   /teachers-biases-girls-education/; Novi Zhukovsky, "Speaking Up
   Gender Imbalance in the Classroom," *Dartmouth*, October 3, 2018,
   https://www.thedartmouth.com/article/2018/10/speaking-up
   -gender-imbalance-in-the-classroom.
6. Uri Gneezy, Kenneth L. Leonard, and John A. List, "Gender
   Differences in Competition: Evidence from a Matrilineal and a
   Patriarchal Society," *Econometrica* 77, no. 5 (September 2009):
   1637–64, https://gap.hks.harvard.edu/gender-differences
   -competition-evidence-matrilineal-and-patriarchal-society.
7. Tyler G. Okimoto and Victoria L. Brescoll, "The Price of Power:
   Power Seeking and Backlash against Female Politicians,"
   Personality and Social Psychology Bulletin 36, no. 7 (2010): 923–36,
   https://doi.org/10.1177/0146167210371949.
8. Michael Kruse, "The Woman Who Made Hillary Cry," *Politico*,
   updated April 21, 2015, https://www.politico.com/story/2015/04
   /the-woman-who-made-hillary-clinton-cry-117171.

9. Annalisa Merelli, "Hillary Clinton Is on 'Humans of New York' Explaining Why She Comes across as Aloof," *Quartz*, updated August 15, 2018, https://qz.com/777077/hillary-clinton-explains-why-shes-unemotional-on-humans-of-new-york/.

10. Sady Doyle, "America Loves Women like Hillary Clinton—as Long as They're Not Asking for a Promotion," Quartz, February 25, 2016, https://qz.com/624346/america-loves-women-like-hillary-clinton-as-long-as-theyre-not-asking-for-a-promotion/.

11. Samantha Grossman, "See the Great Advice Mark Zuckerberg Gave a Facebook Commenter," *Time*, January 4, 2016, https://time.com/4166007/mark-zuckerberg-advice-date-nerd/.

12. Nick Anderson, "Research Shows Young Girls Are Less Likely to Think of Women as 'Really, Really Smart'," *Washington Post*, January 26, 2017, https://www.washingtonpost.com/news/grade-point/wp/2017/01/26/research-shows-young-girls-are-less-likely-to-think-of-women-as-really-really-smart/.

13. Dani Matias, "New Report Says College-Educated Women Will Soon Make Up Majority of U.S. Labor Force," *NWPB*, June 20, 2019, https://www.nwpb.org/2019/06/20/new-report-says-college-educated-women-will-soon-make-up-majority-of-u-s-labor-force/.

14. Margarita Mayo, "To Seem Confident, Women Have to Be Seen as Warm," *Harvard Business Review*, July 8, 2016, https://hbr.org/2016/07/to-seem-confident-women-have-to-be-seen-as-warm.

15. Jo Paoletti, "What's Wrong with Gender Stereotypes?," *Pink Is for Boys* (blog), June 12, 2012, https://www.pinkisforboys.org/blog/whats-wrong-with-gender-stereotypes.

16. Sociologists for Women in Society, "Gender Bias Uncovered in Children's Books with Male Characters, Including Male Animals, Leading the Fictional Pack," *ScienceDaily*, May 4, 2011, www.sciencedaily.com/releases/2011/05/110503151607.htm.

17. "Brontë Family," Wikipedia, accessed February 3, 2022, https://en.wikipedia.org/wiki/Bront%C3%AB_family.

18. Emma Cueto, "Why Is J.K. Still Pretending to Write as a Man?," *Bustle*, February 18, 2014, https://www.bustle.com/articles/15839-what-jk-rowling-using-a-male-pseudonym-says-about-sexism-in-publishing.

19. Drew Desilver, "Women Scarce at Top of U.S. Business—And in the

Jobs That Lead There," PEW Research Center, April 30, 2018, https://www.pewresearch.org/fact-tank/2018/04/30/women -scarce-at-top-of-u-s-business-and-in-the-jobs-that-lead-there/.

20. "Female to Male Earnings Ratio of Workers in the U.S. in Q4 2020, by Age Group," Statista, January 2021, https://www.statista.com/ statistics/244383/female-to-male-earnings-ratio-of-workers-in-the -us-by-age/.

21. Jess Huang et al., "Women in the Workplace 2021," *McKinsey & Company*, September 27, 2021, https://www.mckinsey.com/featured -insights/diversity-and-inclusion/women-in-the-workplace.

22. Jennifer L. Prewitt-Freilino, T. Andrew Caswell, and Emmi K. Laakso, "The Gendering of Language: A Comparison of Gender Equality in Countries with Gendered, Natural Gender, and Genderless Languages," *Sex Roles* 66 (2012): 268–81, https://doi.org/10.1007 /s11199-011-0083-5.

23. Klint Finley, "New Study Exposes Gender Bias in Tech Job Listings," *Wired*, March 11, 2013, https://www.wired.com/2013/03/hiring -women/.

24. Cid Wilson et al., "Missing Pieces Report: The 2018 Board Diversity Census of Women and Minorities on Fortune 500 Boards," Harvard Law School Forum on Corporate Governance, February 5, 2019, https://corpgov.law.harvard.edu/2019/02/05/missing-pieces-report -the-2018-board-diversity-census-of-women-and-minorities-on -fortune-500-boards/#3b.

25. Kim Elsesser, "What to Expect from the Influx of Women on California's Corporate Boards," *Forbes*, May 21, 2021, https://www .forbes.com/sites/kimelsesser/2021/05/21/what-to-expect-from-the -influx-of-women-on-californias-corporate-boards/?sh=7e93f0bc12ce.

26. Jeffrey Dastin, "Amazon Scraps Secret AI Recruiting Tool That Showed Bias against Women," *Reuters*, October 10, 2018, https:// www.reuters.com/article/us-amazon-com-jobs-automation -insight-idUSKCN1MK08G.

27. Dave Gershgorn, "Robot Indemnity: Companies Are on the Hook If Their Hiring Algorithms Are Biased," *Quartz*, last updated October 23, 2018, https://qz.com/1427621/companies-are-on-the-hook-if -their-hiring-algorithms-are-biased/.

28. Kieran Snyder, "The Abrasiveness Trap: High-Achieving Men and

Women Are Described Differently in Reviews," Stanford Medicine Diversity Initiative, Stanford University, August 26, 2014, 3, https://web.stanford.edu/dept/radiology/cgi-bin/raddiversity/wp-content/uploads/2017/12/TheAbrasivenessTrap.pdf.

29. Malin Malmström, Jeaneth Johansson, and Joakim Wincent, "Gender Stereotypes and Venture Support Decisions: How Governmental Venture Capitalists Socially Construct Entrepreneurs' Potential," *Entrepreneurship Theory and Practice* 41, no. 5 (September 2017): 833–60, https://doi.org/10.1111/etap.12275.

30. Kate Clark, "US VC Investment in Female Founders Hits All-Time High," TechCrunch, December 9, 2019, https://techcrunch.com/2019/12/09/us-vc-investment-in-female-founders-hits-all-time-high/.

31. Johannes Lenhard, "Inside VC Firms: The Gender Divide," CrunchBase, August 14, 2019, https://news.crunchbase.com/news/inside-vc-firms-the-gender-divide/.

32. Katie Abouzahr et al., "Why Women-Owned Startups Are a Better Bet," BCG, June 6, 2018, https://www.bcg.com/en-us/publications/2018/why-women-owned-startups-are-better-bet.

33. Paul A. Gompers and Sophie Q. Wang, "And the Children Shall Lead: Gender Diversity and Performance in Venture Capital," (working paper, *National Bureau of Economic Research*, Cambridge, MA, May 2017), https://doi.org/10.3386/w23454.

34. University of British Columbia, "Hiring Committees That Don't Believe in Gender Bias Promote Fewer Women," *Science Daily*, August 26, 2019, https://www.sciencedaily.com/releases/2019/08/190826112653.htm.

35. Stefanie K. Johnson, David R. Hekman, and Elsa T. Chan, "If There's Only One Woman in Your Candidate Pool, There's Statistically No Chance She'll Be Hired," *Harvard Business Review*, April 26, 2016, https://hbr.org/2016/04/if-theres-only-one-woman-in-your-candidate-pool-theres-statistically-no-chance-shell-be-hired.

36. "How Big Is the Wage Penalty for Mothers?," *Economist*, January 28, 2019, https://www.economist.com/graphic-detail/2019/01/28/how-big-is-the-wage-penalty-for-mothers.

37. Sarah Kliff, "The Truth about the Gender Wage Gap," Vox,

September 18, 2017, https://www.vox.com/2017/9/8/16268362 /gender-wage-gap-explained.

38. Claire Cain Miller, "Nearly Half of Men Say They Do Most of the Home Schooling. 3 Percent of Women Agree," *New York Times*, updated May 8, 2020, https://www.nytimes.com/2020/05/06/upshot/pandemic -chores-homeschooling-gender.html. See: Who is spending more time home-schooling your children or helping them with distance learning?

39. Shelley J. Correll, Stephen Benard, and In Paik, "Getting a Job: Is There a Motherhood Penalty?," *American Journal of Sociology* 112, no. 5 (March 2007): 1297–338, https://doi.org/10.1086/511799.

40. Natalie Gontcharova, "5 Women Share Their Stories of Pregnancy Discrimination," Refinery29, updated October 11, 2019, https://www .refinery29.com/en-us/2019/10/8563273/elizabeth-warren -pregnancy-discrimination-stories.

41. Sarah Jane Glynn, "Breadwinning Mothers Continue to Be the U.S. Norm," Center for American Progress, May 10, 2019, https://www .americanprogress.org/article/breadwinning-mothers-continue -u-s-norm/.

42. Claire Cain Miller, "The Motherhood Penalty vs. the Fatherhood Bonus," *New York Times*, September 6, 2014, https://www.nytimes .com/2014/09/07/upshot/a-child-helps-your-career-if-youre-a-man .html?_r=0.

43. Andrew Moravcsik, "Why I Put My Wife's Career First," *Atlantic*, October 2015, https://www.theatlantic.com/magazine/archive /2015/10/why-i-put-my-wifes-career-first/403240/.

44. Sylvia Ann Hewlett, Carolyn Buck Luce, and Lisa J. Servon, "Stopping the Exodus of Women in Science," *Harvard Business Review*, June 2008, https://hbr.org/2008/06/stopping-the-exodus-of-women-in -science.

Rule #2: Don't Give Yourself a Free Pass

1. Burton W. Kanter, "AARP—Asset Accumulation, Retention and Protection," *Taxes* 69 (1991): 717.

2. Albert Mehrabian and Alan Chapman, "Mehrabian's Communication Theory: Verbal, Non-Verbal, Body Language," BusinessBalls, updated October 13, 2021, https://www.businessballs.com/

communication-skills/mehrabians-communication-theory-verbal-non-verbal-body-language/.

3. Mehrabian and Chapman, "Mehrabian's Communication Theory."

4. Wikipedia, s.v. "A Better Chance," last modified September 13, 2021, https://en.wikipedia.org/wiki/A_Better_Chance.

5. "Exeter, New Hampshire," Wikipedia, accessed February 3, 2022, https://en.wikipedia.org/wiki/Exeter,_New_Hampshire.

6. "One of the Largest Latina-Led Funds in the US, Ulu Ventures, Raises $138M for Its Third Fund," *Business Wire*, May 17, 2021, https://www.businesswire.com/news/home/20210517005200/en/One-of-the-Largest-Latina-Led-Funds-in-the-US-Ulu-Ventures-Raises-138M-for-its-Third-Fund.

7. "Maeley Tom: Trailblazer in Asian American Politics," Committee of 100, accessed November 27, 2021, https://www.committee100.org/member/maeleytom/.

Rule #3: Chart Your Own Course

1. Aparna Dhinakaran, "The Journey to Fairness in AI: Q&A with New York Times Best Selling Author Abigail Hing Wen," *Forbes*, June 28, 2021, https://www.forbes.com/sites/aparnadhinakaran/2021/06/28/the-journey-to-fairness-in-aiqa-with-new-york-times-best-selling-author-abigail-hing-wen/?sh=277a360a4ad3.

2. *Goals Research Summary*, Dominican Education, February 2020, https://www.dominican.edu/sites/default/files/2020-02/gailmatthews-harvard-goals-researchsummary.pdf.

3. Dashun Wang and Benjamin F. Jones, "When Losing Out on a Big Opportunity Helps Your Career," *Harvard Business Review*, October 1, 2019, https://hbr.org/2019/10/research-when-losing-out-on-a-big-opportunity-helps-your-career.

4. "Dr. Sapna Cheryan invited to the White House," University of Washington Department of Psychology, accessed January 14, 2022, https://psych.uw.edu/newsletter/winter-2016/faculty-focus/dr-sapna-cheryan-invited-to-the-white-house.

5. Lisa Grossman, "Stereotypes Steer Women Away from Computer Science," *ScienceNews*, December 15, 2009, https://web.archive.org/web/20091218165825/https://www

.sciencenews.org/view/generic/id/50804/title/Stereotypes_steer
_women_away_from_computer_science.

6. Doree Armstrong, "More Women Pick Computer Science If Media Nix Outdated 'Nerd' Stereotype," University of Washington, June 25, 2013, https://www.washington.edu/news/2013/06/25/more-women -pick-computer-science-if-media-nix-outdated-nerd-stereotype/.

Rule #4: Build a Learning Mindset

1. "KPMG Study Finds 75% of Female Executives across Industries Have Experienced Imposter Syndrome in Their Careers," KPMG, October 7, 2020, https://info.kpmg.us/news-perspectives/people -culture/kpmg-study-finds-most-female-executives-experience -imposter-syndrome.html.

2. "What a Marshmallow Reveals about Collaboration," *Inc.*, October 7, 2020, https://www.inc.com/the-build-network/build-a-tower-build -a-team.html.

3. Lisa Abeyta, "Women Now Make up Almost 5 Percent of Investors in the U.S.," *Inc.*, October 23, 2020, https://www.inc.com/lisa-abeyta /women-now-make-up-almost-five-percent-of-investors-in-us.html.

4. Katie Benner, "A Backlash Builds against Sexual Harassment in Silicon Valley," *New York Times*, July 3, 2017, https://www.nytimes .com/2017/07/03/technology/silicon-valley-sexual-harassment.html.

5. Dave McClure, "I'm a Creep. I'm Sorry.," 500 Hats, July 1, 2017, https://web.archive.org/web/20170702005224if_/https://500hats .com/im-a-creep-i-m-sorry-d2c13e996ea0.

6. Emma Hinchliffe, "Bumble CEO Whitney Wolfe Herd Becomes the Youngest Woman to Take a Company Public," *Fortune*, February 11, 2021, https://fortune.com/2021/02/11/bumble-ipo-ceo-whitney -wolfe-herd-bmbl-stock-shares-interview-app-initial-public-offering/.

7. Lisa Bonos, "Why Are Tinder and Bumble Fighting? Here's Everything You Need to Know," *Washington Post*, updated March 22, 2018, https://www.washingtonpost.com/news/soloish/wp/2018 /03/22/why-are-tinder-and-bumble-fighting-its-been-a-long-and -winding-feud/.

8. Sara Ashley O'Brien, "She Sued Tinder, Founded Bumble and Now, at 30, Is the CEO of a $3 Billion Dating Empire," *CNN*, December 13, 2019, https://www.cnn.com/2019/12/13/tech/whitney-wolfe-herd

-bumble-risk-takers/index.html; "Bumble Inc. Announces First Quarter 2021 Results," Bumble, May 12, 2021, https://ir.bumble.com /node/7046/pdf.

9. Bonos, "Tinder and Bumble."

10. Jeremy Kahn, "Bumble Parent Told to Implement Workplace Reforms after Sexism Allegations," *Fortune*, January 30, 2020, https:// fortune.com/2020/01/30/magiclab-bumble-sexism-allegations -workplace-reforms/.

11. Tim Bower, "Why Rookie CEOs Outperform," *Harvard Business Review*, January–February 2021, https://hbr.org/2021/01/why-rookie -ceos-outperform.

Rule #5: Learn to Forgive

1. Kirsten Fiscus, "'I Forgive You': Emanuel AME Church Survivor, Widow Speak on Forgiveness Following 2015 Shooting," *Montgomery Advertiser*, updated May 7, 2019, https://www.montgomeryadvertiser .com/story/news/crime/2019/05/06/charleston-shooting-survivor -widow-preach-forgiveness-montgomery-church/1117237001/.

2. Matt Shiavenza, "Hatred and Forgiveness in Charleston," *Atlantic*, June 20, 2015, https://www.theatlantic.com/national/archive /2015/06/dylann-roof-manifesto-forgiveness/396428/.

3. "Awaiting Speeches by Biden, Kaine & Obama at the Democratic National Convention," CNN Live Event/Special, Aired July 27, 2016, on CNN, https://transcripts.cnn.com/show/se/date/2016-07-27 /segment/02.

4. Loren Toussaint et al., "Effects of Lifetime Stress Exposure on Mental and Physical Health in Young Adulthood: How Stress Degrades and Forgiveness Protects Health," *Journal of Health Psychology* 21, no. 6 (June 2016): 1004–14, https://doi.org/10.1177 /1359105314544132.

5. Kirsten Weir, "Forgiveness Can Improve Mental and Physical Health: Research Shows How to Get There," *American Psychological Association* 48, no. 1 (January 2017): 30, https://www.apa.org /monitor/2017/01/ce-corner.

6. Rowena Chiu, "Harvey Weinstein Told Me He Liked Chinese Girls," *New York Times*, October 5, 2019, https://www.nytimes.com/2019 /10/05/opinion/sunday/harvey-weinstein-rowena-chiu.html.

7. Jonah E. Bromwich, "Harvey Weinstein Appeals Sex Crimes Conviction Over Accusers' Testimony," *New York Times*, April 5, 2021, https://www.nytimes.com/2021/04/05/nyregion/harvey-weinstein -appeal.html.

8. Debbie Elliott, "Dylann Roof Found Guilty of All Counts of Killing 9 Black Worshippers," *NPR*, December 15, 2016, https://www.npr.org /2016/12/15/505751251/dylann-roof-found-guilty-of-all-counts-of -killing-9-black-worshippers; Rebecca Hersher, "Dylann Roof Sentenced to Death," *NPR*, January 10, 2017, https://www.npr.org /sections/thetwo-way/2017/01/10/509166866/jury-sentences -dylann-roof-to-die.

9. Loren Toussaint et al., "Is Forgiveness One of the Secrets to Success? Considering the Costs of Workplace Disharmony and the Benefits of Teaching Employees to Forgive," *American Journal of Health Promotion* 33, no. 7 (September 2019): 1090–3, https://doi.org/10.1177 /0890117119866957e.

Rule #6: Develop Allies

1. Lexico, s.v. "mentor," accessed January 21, 2022, https://www.lexico .com/en/definition/mentor.

2. B. R. J. O'Donnell, "*The Odyssey*'s Millennia-Old Model of Mentorship," *Atlantic*, October 13, 2017, https://www.theatlantic .com/business/archive/2017/10/the-odyssey-mentorship/542676/.

3. Stephanie Neal, Jazmine Boatman, and Linda Miller, *Women as Mentors: Does She or Doesn't She,* Development Dimensions International, 2013, 5, https://media.ddiworld.com/research /women-as-mentors_research_ddi.pdf.

4. Gene Pease, "Appendix E: Mentoring Case Study," in *Optimize Your Greatest Asset—Your People: How to Apply Analytics to Big Data to Improve Your Human Capital Investments* (Hoboken, NJ: John Wiley & Sons, 2015), 165, https://onlinelibrary.wiley.com/doi/pdf/10.1002 /9781119040002.app5.

5. Naz Beheshti, "Improve Workplace Culture with a Strong Mentoring Program," *Forbes*, January 23, 2019, https://www.forbes.com/sites /nazbeheshti/2019/01/23/improve-workplace-culture-with-a-strong -mentoring-program/?sh=40eb9eff76b5.

6. Lexico, s.v. "sponsor," accessed November 22, 2021, https://www
.lexico.com/en/definition/sponsor.

7. Sylvia Ann Hewlett, *Forget a Mentor, Find a Sponsor: The New Way
to Fast-Track Your Career* (Boston: Harvard Business Review Press,
2013), 24.

8. "Working Relationships in the #MeToo Era," Lean In, accessed
December 2, 2021, https://leanin.org/sexual-harassment-backlash
-survey-results.

9. David A. Matsa and Amalia R. Miller, "Chipping Away at the Glass
Ceiling: Gender Spillovers in Corporate Leadership" (RAND Labor
and Population Working Paper Series, Santa Monica, CA, 2011),
https://papers.ssrn.com/sol3/papers.cfm?abstract_id=1799575.

10. Michelle Duguid, "Female Tokens in High-Prestige Work Groups:
Catalysts or Inhibitors of Group Diversification?," *Organizational
Behavior and Human Decision Processes* 116, no. 1 (September 2011):
104–115, https://doi.org/10.1016/j.obhdp.2011.05.009.

11. Stefanie K. Johnson and David R. Hekman, "Women and Minorities
Are Penalized for Promoting Diversity," *Harvard Business Review*,
March 23, 2016, https://hbr.org/2016/03/women-and-minorities
-are-penalized-for-promoting-diversity.

12. *Merriam-Webster*, s.v. "team," accessed January 14, 2022, https://
www.merriam-webster.com/dictionary/team.

13. Julia Rozovsky, "The Five Keys to a Successful Google Team,"
LinkedIn, November 18, 2015, https://www.linkedin.com/pulse
/five-keys-successful-google-team-laszlo-bock/.

14. Lexico, s.v. "circle," accessed February 5, 2022, https://www.lexico
.com/en/definition/circle.

Rule #7: Embrace Who You Are

1. Hannah Collins, "Marvel Studios Still Doesn't Think Women Can
Lead Solo Films," CBR, August 18, 2019, https://www.cbr.com
/marvel-studios-solo-women-films/.

2. Deb Liu, "The Right Words for the Job: How Gendered Language
Affects the Workplace," *Medium*, February 25, 2017, https://medium
.com/women-in-product/genderwords-b0be0cc8251f.

3. David Sadker, Myra Sadker, and Karen Zittleman, "The Beginning of
the Classroom Compromise: The Elementary School Years," in *Still*

Failing at Fairness: How Gender Bias Cheats Girls and Boys in School and What We Can Do About It, 2nd ed. (New York: Scribner, 2009).

4. Victor Lavy and Edith Sand, "On the Origins of Gender Human Capital Gaps: Short and Long Term Consequences of Teachers' Stereotypical Biases" (NBER Working Paper Series, National Bureau of Economic Research, Cambridge, MA, January 2015), https://www .nber.org/system/files/working_papers/w20909/w20909.pdf.

5. Yasemin Copur-Gencturk et al., "Teachers' Bias against the Mathematical Ability of Female, Black, and Hispanic Students," *Educational Researcher* 49, no. 1 (January 2020): 30–43, https://doi .org/10.3102/0013189X19890577.

6. Shelley J. Correll and Caroline Simard, "Research: Vague Feedback Is Holding Women Back," *Harvard Business Review*, April 29, 2016, https://hbr.org/2016/04/research-vague-feedback-is-holding -women-back.

7. Kieran Snyder, "The Abrasiveness Trap: High-Achieving Men and Women Are Described Differently in Reviews," Stanford Medicine Diversity Initiative, Stanford University, August 26, 2014, 1–4, https://web.stanford.edu/dept/radiology/cgi-bin/raddiversity/wp -content/uploads/2017/12/TheAbrasivenessTrap.pdf.

8. "Interpersonal Dynamics," Stanford Graduate School of Business, accessed December 2, 2021, https://www.gsb.stanford.edu /experience/learning/leadership/interpersonal-dynamics.

9. Marc Ethier, "Inside 'Touchy Feely,' Stanford's Iconic MBA Course," Poets & Quants, July 22, 2018, https://poetsandquants.com/2018/07 /22/inside-touchy-feely-stanfords-iconic-mba-course/.

10. "Changing the Curve: Women in Computing," UC Berkeley School of Information, July 14, 2021, https://ischoolonline.berkeley.edu/blog /women-computing-computer-science/.

11. Deborah Liu, "What Happened to Women in Product?," LinkedIn, October 21, 2020, accessed February 3, 2022, https://www.linkedin .com/pulse/what-happened-women-product-deborah-liu/.

Rule #8: Create Balance at Home

1. "The Second Shift," Wikipedia, accessed February 4, 2022, https:// en.wikipedia.org/wiki/The_Second_Shift.

2. Anna Hecht, "Here's How Much the Average Wedding Cost in 2019,"

CNBC, February 14, 2020, https://www.cnbc.com/2020/02/13/how
-much-the-average-wedding-cost-in-2019.html; Anna Hecht, "10
US States Where Couples Spend More than 45% of Their Income on
Their Wedding," CNBC, September 6, 2019, https://www.cnbc.com
/2019/09/06/us-states-where-couples-spend-nearly-half-of-their
-income-on-their-wedding.html.

3. Maddy Sims, "Here's the Average Length of Engagement for Couples,"
The Knot, June 14, 2020, https://www.theknot.com/content/too
-long-to-be-engaged.

4. Drew Weisholtz, "Women Do 2 More Hours of Housework Daily than
Men, Study Says," *Today*, January 22, 2020, https://www.today.com
/news/women-do-2-more-hours-housework-daily-men-study-says
-t172272.

5. Sarah Jane Glynn, "An Unequal Division of Labor: How Equitable
Workplace Policies Would Benefit Working Mothers," Center for
American Progress, May 18, 2018, https://americanprogress.org
/article/unequal-division-labor/.

6. Katie Abouzahr et al., "Dispelling the Myths of the Gender 'Ambition
Gap,'" The Boston Consulting Group, April 2017, https://www.bcg
.com/publications/2017/people-organization-leadership-change
-dispelling-the-myths-of-the-gender-ambition-gap.

7. "How Big Is the Wage Penalty for Mothers?," *Economist*, January 28,
2019, https://www.economist.com/graphic-detail/2019/01/28/how
-big-is-the-wage-penalty-for-mothers.

8. Anne-Marie Slaughter, "Why Women Still Can't Have It All," *Atlantic*,
July 2012, https://www.theatlantic.com/magazine/archive/2012/07
/why-women-still-cant-have-it-all/309020/.

9. Andrew Moravcsik, "Why I Put My Wife's Career First," *Atlantic*,
October 2015, https://www.theatlantic.com/magazine/archive
/2015/10/why-i-put-my-wifes-career-first/403240/.

10. "New Research Shows the 'Mental Load' Is Real and Significantly
Impacts Working Mothers Both at Home and Work," Bright
Horizons, December 20, 2017, https://www.brighthorizons.com
/newsroom/mental-load-impact-working-mothers-study.

11. Emma Hinchliffe, "Married Women Do More Housework than Single
Moms, Study Finds," *Fortune*, May 8, 2019, https://fortune.com/2019
/05/08/married-single-moms-housework/.

12. Wikipedia, s.v. "Swim lane," last modified May 11, 2021, https://en.wikipedia.org/wiki/Swim_lane.

13. Glynn, "An Unequal Division of Labor."

14. Aliya Hamid Rao, "Even Breadwinning Wives Don't Get Equality at Home," *Atlantic*, May 16, 2019, https://www.theatlantic.com/family/archive/2019/05/breadwinning-wives-gender-inequality/589237/.

15. Don Lee, "Women Put Careers on Hold during COVID to Care for Kids. They May Never Recover," *Los Angeles Times*, August 18, 2021, https://www.latimes.com/politics/story/2021-08-18/pandemic-pushes-moms-to-scale-back-or-quit-their-careers.

Rule #9: Find Your Voice

1. Alison Mitchell, "Peculiar Passages: The Case of Ruth, Boaz and the Contractual Sandal," The Good Book, August 15, 2019, https://www.thegoodbook.com/blog/interestingthoughts/2019/08/15/peculiar-passages-the-case-of-ruth-boaz-and-the-co/.

2. Kate Clark, "US VC Investment in Female Founders Hits All-Time High," TechCrunch, December 9, 2019, https://techcrunch.com/2019/12/09/us-vc-investment-in-female-founders-hits-all-time-high/.

3. Wikipedia, s.v. "Pao v. Kleiner Perkins," last modified November 22, 2021, https://en.wikipedia.org/wiki/Pao_v._Kleiner_Perkins.

4. Pavithra Mohan, "This Is How We Get More Women in Venture Capital," *Fast Company*, September 20, 2018, https://www.fastcompany.com/90233436/this-is-how-we-get-more-women-in-venture-capital.

5. Aileen Lee, "Announcing AllRaise.org," *Medium*, April 3, 2018, https://medium.com/allraise/announcing-allraise-org-d15a1b592f63.

6. Aileen Lee, "Welcome to the Unicorn Club: Learning from Billion-Dollar Startups," TechCrunch, November 2, 2013, https://techcrunch.com/2013/11/02/welcome-to-the-unicorn-club/.

7. J. Carlisle Larsen, "Study Shows Female Supreme Court Justices Get Interrupted More Often than Male Colleagues: Expert Says These Interruptions Can Have an Impact on Rulings and Undermine Female Justices," Wisconsin Public Radio, April 18, 2017, https://www.wpr.org/study-shows-female-supreme-court-justices-get-interrupted-more-often-male-colleagues.

8. Lydia Smith, "The Stark Reality of How Men Dominate Talking in

Meetings," Yahoo! Finance, April 10, 2019, https://finance.yahoo.com /news/stark-reality-men-dominate-talking-meetings-113112910.html.

9. Kathy Caprino, "Gender Bias Is Real: Women's Perceived Competency Drops Significantly When Judged as Being Forceful," *Forbes*, August 25, 2015, https://www.forbes.com/sites/kathycaprino/2015/08/25 /gender-bias-is-real-womens-perceived-competency-drops -significantly-when-judged-as-being-forceful/?sh=3384f36b2d85.

10. Victoria L. Brescoll, "Who Takes the Floor and Why: Gender, Power, and Volubility in Organizations," *Administrative Science Quarterly* 56, no. 4 (2011): 622–41, https://doi.org/10.1177/0001839212439994.

11. Brittany Karford Rogers, "When Women Don't Speak: Ground-breaking BYU Research Shows What It Takes for a Woman to Truly Be Heard," *Y Magazine*, Spring 2020, https://magazine.byu.edu /article/when-women-dont-speak/.

12. Wikipedia, s.v. "PayPal Mafia," last modified December 10, 2021, https://en.wikipedia.org/wiki/PayPal_Mafia.

Rule #10: Make Your Mark

1. Columbia *Crew Survival Investigation Report*, NASA, 2008, https:// www.nasa.gov/pdf/298870main_SP-2008-565.pdf.

2. *Growth & Opportunity Project*, Republican National Committee, March 2013, https://online.wsj.com/public/resources/documents /RNCreport03182013.pdf.

3. "Appendiceal Cancer," National Cancer Institute, accessed January 21, 2022, https://www.cancer.gov/pediatric-adult-rare-tumor/rare -tumors/rare-digestive-system-tumors/appendiceal-cancer.

4. "Appendix Cancer," MD Anderson Cancer Center Madrid, accessed January 21, 2022, https://mdanderson.es/en/cancer/cancerfromatoz /appendix-cancer.

5. "Surgical Treatment of Appendix Cancer Cytoreduction and HIPEC," Appendix Cancer Connection, accessed December 3, 2021, https:// appendix-cancer.org/surgical-treatment-of-appendix-cancer/.

6. Anne CC Lee et al., "A Novel Icterometer for Hyperbilirubinemia Screening in Low-Resource Settings," *Pediatrics* 143, no. 5 (May 2019), https://doi.org/10.1542/peds.2018-2039.

7. Carolyn Everson, "Facebook's Carolyn Everson: Why Writing a Personal Vision Statement Has Been Game-Changing for Me,"

Thrive Global, December 1, 2016, https://medium.com/thrive
-global/facebooks-carolyn-everson-why-writing-a-vision-has-been
-game-changing-for-me-c7271093fc47.

8. "AOL Agrees to Acquire the Huffington Post," *Huffington Post*,
updated May 25, 2011, https://www.huffpost.com/entry/aol
-huffington-post_n_819375.

From the Publisher

GREAT BOOKS

ARE EVEN BETTER WHEN THEY'RE SHARED!

Help other readers find this one

- Post a review at your favorite online bookseller

- Post a picture on a social media account and share why you enjoyed it

- Send a note to a friend who would also love it—or better yet, give them a copy

Thanks for reading!